Kristofferson and Yeats

Finding Christ in Verse

by

Gregg Tomusko

Published in the United States of America
ISBN-13: 978-1719021470
ISBN-10: 1719021473

Other books by Gregg Tomusko:

Two Lessons of Jesus, Jesus Never Said That!
The War For Minds
College Math for Children
Why Do Doggies Smile? What If? What's For Dinner?
What You'd Buy Me? How Puerile!

All can be found on Amazon.com

All children are mine
and no child is mine

Attributed to Michael O. Boyce, Esoteric Astrologer and friend

Dedicated to the US Armed Forces, with the pure
motive of making the world a safer place.

Author's Note: This book was released on November 7, 2016, the day Leonard Cohen
passed. I had hoped he would see this tribute to him.

I hope some of my favorite artists see this book, as they have given me a lifetime of
inspiration and joy. I believe all the names within belong together, having labored well
and leaving this world an entrance into truth, beauty, and goodness: the attributes of
God.

End of Summer Discussion

The End

INTRODUCTION

I am a teacher. No matter what career I find myself in, I teach. *Teacher* is more than a profession, it defines a type of soul. If you are cheered by meaningful measures crafted in beauty, then you possess a teacher's soul. Teachers tend to give of themselves. They love to share with others what they know.

I gained my appreciation of verse from a priest who was an English professor and a great teacher. He seemed to know why I didn't like literature, and won me over by observing, "Truth, beauty, and goodness are objective." I didn't like English because I found it subjective.

In high school, we all enjoyed songs, but didn't like poetry. If we'd known that a popular tune's inception began with the artist's reading of a poem, we might have taken a second look. It takes a lot of talent to write a song. The seed contains a poem:

"earth by april"
   — anyone lived in a pretty how town by E.E. Cummings
E.E. Cummings referring to April as an interior decorator of earth may have inspired D. Loggins to pen Pieces of April.

"What have you to do with the mysteries
Of this ancient place, of my ancient curse?"
   — Under the Oak by D. H. Lawrence
"And your long-time curse hurts"
   —Just Like a Woman by Bob Dylan

"Come live with me and be my love"
   — The Passionate Shepherd to His Love by Christopher Marlowe
   — This line became a song, written by Felice and Boudleaux Bryant, and a hit
      record for Roy Clark.

I read poetry today for enjoyment and escape. I've always liked songs, especially if they have good lyrics. This book contains my favorites, both songs and poems. I hope you like them too.

We all need inspiration, and a means to participate in what uplifts us spiritually. There's got to be more. Our desires for value, for truth, beauty, and goodness, for adventure and gold, serve not as misguided, impractical impulses but rather a door that—if we knock—will open. Once we enter, we lose our desire to ever return. We find happiness.

Some of my selections differ from other anthologies. I expanded the scope to include songs, which I view as poems set to music. I first look at the lyrics, and then enjoy these words enhanced with music that helps me emotionally experience each one more fully.

Some selections missed being the artists' most popular. No recording artist repeats the same songs on every album, but rather offers something original. Playing only past bestsellers may reduce the audience's interest.

There's something exciting in discovery, as a poem that wends a pathway less taken into our soul or recognizes an old truth in a new way. The poem may be lacking in beauty, but excel in truth; naive, but touch us with goodness. I look for spiritual qualities that uplift, and for revelations that leave me nodding in agreement. "I know just what you mean. I've lived through the same thing. If I had not experienced that, I don't think I'd appreciate the full impact of your poem—the reserved emotions and careful choice of words."

Truth, beauty, and goodness exist as objective realities, and outlast the poet's days of breathing. We discover, rediscover, and pen today many creative works. The best ought to be collected, savored, and preserved in a book to inspire generations.

Many of the masters shine on these pages. Their works may yet illuminate a new discovery within our soul, even though we've struggled through an exhaustive study in googols of English classes!

John Keats, on reading Chapman's *Homer*, discovers a classic as if for the first time. He involves our senses in the enjoyment, and does so with controlled enthusiasm.

ON FIRST LOOKING INTO CHAPMAN'S HOMER

Much have I traveled in the realms of gold,
    And many goodly states and kingdoms seen;
    Round many western islands have I been
Which bards in fealty to Apollo hold.
Oft of one wide expanse had I been told
    That deep-browed Homer ruled as his demesne;
    Yet did I never breathe its pure serene
Till I heard Chapman speak out loud and bold:
Then felt I like some watcher of the skies
    When a new planet swims into his ken;
Or like stout Cortez when with eagle eyes
    He stared at the Pacific—and all his men
Looked at each other with a wild surmise—
    Silent, upon a peak in Darien.

We may not appreciate the full mastery of contemporary artists. We experience difficulty in determining whether a work will stand the test of time. Some rise relevant only today, yet, if I've helped even one man, what an accomplishment.

Some of my choices do not necessarily include the best. This begins as a curious line of consultation! From an academic stance, the images are not the most crisp, the sources taken from the rich storehouses of classical literature, or the artistry subtle and profound. Yet, there come emotional, sad, and down-and-out times where simple, heartfelt, common human experiences answers what we're after—a kindred spirit, a friend to help.

Henry Wadsworth Longfellow expressed this in his song "The Day Is Done." He included this in a collection of poems he called *The Waif*.

Gregg Tomusko

SONGS
THE DAY IS DONE

The day is done, and the darkness
    Falls from the wings of Night,
As a feather is wafted downward
    From an eagle in his flight.

I see the lights of the village
    Gleam through the rain and the mist,
And a feeling of sadness comes o'er me
    That my soul cannot resist:

A feeling of sadness and longing,
    That is not akin to pain,
And resembles sorrow only
    As the mist resembles the rain.

Come, read to me some poem,
    Some simple and heartfelt lay,
That shall soothe this restless feeling,
    And banish the thoughts of day.

Not from the grand old masters,
    Not from the bards sublime,
Whose distant footsteps echo
    Through the corridors of Time.

For, like strains of martial music,
    Their mighty thoughts suggest
Life's endless toil and endeavor;
    And tonight I long for rest.

Read from some humbler poet,
    Whose songs gushed from his heart,
As showers from the clouds of summer,
    Or tears from the eyelids start;

Who, through long days of labor,
    And nights devoid of ease,
Still heard in his soul the music
    Of wonderful melodies.

Such songs have power to quiet
    The restless pulse of care,
And come like the benediction
    That follows after prayer.

Then read from the treasured volume
    The poem of thy choice,
And lend to the rhyme of the poet
    The beauty of thy voice.

And the night shall be filled with music,
    And the cares, that infest the day,
Shall fold their tents, like the Arabs,
    And as silently steal away.

Henry Wadsworth Longfellow became known as the "children's poet." Can there be a higher compliment? I'd bet visitors feel welcome in his home.

Well, Mr. Longfellow insists that we stay for dinner. I'd best explain what so attracted me that I boldly knocked on his, and others', front doors! Additionally, any community meetings or parties we will, of course, attend! Please jot down all the attached dates, since I took the liberty of also inviting you.

We both know some English classes resemble torture! We analyze poems for hidden meanings and employ critics to figure what the poet attempted to say and decipher symbols he alone used. We admittedly became impressed with the way poets stated certain truths. Since some struck the right chord, we remember them fondly, and wish to return to "better times." Poetry played a part in those times.

This collection we can view as a second visit. We don't have to pass a test. We try to satisfy our life's quest for truth, beauty, and goodness. Your journey favors selections I missed or dismissed as "not impressed." Each poet reaches out to us with a different orchestration of words and sounds to help make us into a masterpiece. Let's go!

September

2

Labor Day

9:00

10:00

11:00

12:00   *Labor Day lecture and luncheon — Glenn's Restaurant*

1:00

2:00

3:00

4:00

5:00

THE EAGLE SOARS IN THE SUMMIT OF HEAVEN
Chorus from *The Rock*

The Eagle soars in the summit of Heaven,
The Hunter with his dogs pursues his circuit.
O perpetual revolution of configured stars,
O perpetual recurrence of determined seasons,
O world of spring and autumn, birth and dying!
The endless cycle of idea and action,
Endless invention, endless experiment,
Brings knowledge of motion, but not of stillness;
Knowledge of speech, but not of silence;
Knowledge of words, and ignorance of the Word.
All our knowledge brings us nearer to our ignorance,
All our ignorance brings us nearer to death,
But nearness to death no nearer to God.
Where is the Life we have lost in living?
Where is the wisdom we have lost in knowledge?
Where is the knowledge we have lost in information?
The cycles of Heaven in twenty centuries
Brings us farther from God and nearer to the Dust.

I journeyed to London, the timekept City,
Where the River flows, with foreign flotations.
There I was told: we have too many churches,
And too few chop-houses. There I was told:
Let the vicars retire, Men do not need the Church
In the place where they work, but where they spend their Sundays.
In the City, we need no bells:
Let them waken the suburbs.
I journeyed to the suburbs, and there I was told:
We toil for six days, on the seventh we must motor
To Hindhead, or Maidenhead.
If the weather is foul we stay at home and read the papers.
In industrial districts, there I was told
Of economic laws.
In the pleasant countryside, there it seemed
That the country now is only fit for picnics.
And the Church does not seem to be wanted
In country or in suburb, and in the town
Only for important weddings.
    T.S. Eliot

Putting too much stock in knowledge, technology, and our many advances can only lead to disaster. We need to remain riveted to God. When we break away, we lose more than we gain.

In this, the computer age, we need to ask:
"Where is the knowledge we have lost in information?"

In this, the secular age, we need to ask:
"Where is the wisdom we have lost in knowledge?"

In this, the busy age, we need to ask:
"Where is the Life we have lost in living?"

Our justification for a church reduced to hosting weddings.

Our labors become endless cycles that spin us away from our foundation. We persist, no longer anchored to a rock, as St. Peter was.

***

Lord,

Thank you for your silence during my trials, for it shows me how little control I have over anything. All comes as a gift from you.

I am busy with everything that ends up being of little importance. Remind me often of what you consider important.

Beautiful churches, built by love, sacrifice, and the labor of our fathers, continue being closed. The carvings in the wood, the gospel scenes out of stained glass, the graceful setting around the altar, lost. We huddle as stupid, faithless men who now face losing you. Help us to see our present condition as "churches closing."

We no longer worship in public, nor do we worship in private. Wake us, so we again hear the church bells calling all men.

SONNET 29

When, in disgrace with fortune and men's eyes,
I all alone beweep my outcast state,
And trouble deaf heaven with my bootless cries,
And look upon myself, and curse my fate,
Wishing me like to one more rich in hope,
Featured like him, like him with friends possessed,
Desiring this man's art and that man's scope,
With what I most enjoy contented least;
Yet in these thoughts myself almost despising,
Haply I think on thee—and then my state,
Like to the lark at break of day arising
From sullen earth, sings hymns at heaven's gate;
For thy sweet love remembered such wealth brings
That then I scorn to change my state with kings.

William Shakespeare

Passed over at work, and prior to that the demeaning experience of the enthusiasm found during an interview followed by a preprinted rejection letter in the mail, becomes very devastating to morale. Others gain success in many things. I seem to be lacking.

The love of a wife, the love God has for us, helps to put failure in perspective. Once renewed, we try again.

***

Lord,

I can't believe the responsibility others take on, and how they seem to learn so much so quickly. I never seem to "get it." My best work involves spending time with you. I don't know why you love me, but I know you do.

Gregg Tomusko

WHEN I HEARD THE LEARN'D ASTRONOMER

When I heard the learn'd astronomer,
When the proofs, the figures, were ranged in columns before me,
When I was shown the charts and diagrams, to add, divide, and measure them,
When I sitting heard the astronomer where he lectured
    with much applause in the lecture-room,
How soon unaccountable I became tired and sick,
Till rising and gliding out I wander'd off by myself,
In the mystical moist night-air, and from time to time,
Look'd up in perfect silence at the stars.

Walt Whitman

It strikes me as amazing how much we know. The reverse is even more amazing: how much we do not know. True learning recognizes how much can be gained through study, and how much more involved life demands of us.

***

Lord,

I'm so thankful I experienced this feeling once; I learned so much mathematics and understood it all, and fully realized I just began. I could have spent a lifetime exploring one fragment of math, and then (hopefully) realize that I still know very little.

I'M NOBODY

I'm nobody! Who are you?
Are you nobody, too?
Then there's a pair of us -- don't tell!
They'd banish us, you know.

How dreary to be somebody!
How public, like a frog
To tell your name the livelong day
To an admiring bog!

Emily Dickinson

We reserve Labor Day as a time to give recognition to the many "nobody's" in the work force, a term many in management feel no discomfiture with. There befall definite advantages and disadvantages to being nobody, just as there come with being somebody.

I walked through the beautiful Brookgreen Gardens in South Carolina, replete with flowers, bearded oaks, lush lawns, inspiring sculpture, poems, fountains like geysers, and glittering bogs, when I came upon Emily's poem carved in marble. It leaps out like a frog! So direct, I felt like someone just poured out their soul to me in seeking a kindred spirit. I wanted to continue our secret conversation!

***

Heavenly Father,

I'm made to feel I'm nobody in the business world. Like a William Shakespeare play, each plot with murderous intent to procure one's slight advantage. Or so it seems to me, achieving little success: a poor player who does his best just to survive.

Yet, I contemplate that I am someone extra special in your eyes.

11

October

9:00   *"The Future" — Town Hall*

10:00   *May take all day*

11:00

12:00

1:00

2:00

3:00

4:00

5:00

THE WORLD IS TOO MUCH WITH US

The world is too much with us; late and soon,
Getting and spending, we lay waste our powers;
Little we see in Nature that is ours;
We have given our hearts away, a sordid boon!
This Sea that bares her bosom to the moon,
The winds that will be howling at all hours,
And are up-gathered now like sleeping flowers,
For this, for everything, we are out of tune;
It moves us not. —Great God! I'd rather be
A Pagan suckled in a creed outworn;
So might I, standing on this pleasant lea,
Have glimpses that would make me less forlorn;
Have sight of Proteus rising from the sea;
Or hear old Triton blow his wreathed horn.

William Wordsworth

Perhaps all our problems add up to, "The world is too much with us." Possessions rule, as we go about getting and spending, and no longer take the time, too blind to be impressed by nature. Has all our progress put us one step behind the pagan?

***

Heavenly Father,

How many warnings do we need that evasions keep us away from you, as Kierkegaard knew a hundred years ago? Work exhausts us, electronic pleasures mesmerize, and we wake tired.

On Sunday I go to Mass, take the dogs to the woods, and relax. I hope we never lose the Lord's Day.

Gregg Tomusko

THE FUTURE

Give me back my broken night
my mirrored room, my secret life
It's lonely here,
there's no one left to torture
Give me absolute control
over every living soul
And lie beside me, baby,
that's an order!

Give me crack and anal sex
Take the only tree that's left
and stuff it up the hole
in your culture
Give me back the Berlin Wall
give me Stalin and St. Paul
I've seen the future, brother:
it is murder.

Things are going to slide in all directions
Won't be nothing
Nothing you can measure any more
The blizzard of the world
has crossed the threshold
and it has overturned
the order of the soul
When they said REPENT
I wonder what they meant

You don't know me from the wind
you never will, you never did
I'm the little jew
who wrote the bible
I've seen the nations rise and fall
I've heard their stories, heard them all
but love's the only engine of survival

Your servant here, he has been told
to say it clear, to say it cold:
It's over, it ain't going
any further

Kristofferson and Yeats

And now the wheels of heaven stop
you feel the devil's riding crop
Get ready for the future:
it is murder.

Things are going to slide in all directions

They'll be the breaking
of the ancient western code
Your private life will suddenly explode
They'll be phantoms
there'll be fires on the road
and the white man dancing
You'll see your woman
hanging upside down
her features covered by her fallen gown
and all the lousy little poets
coming round
trying to sound like Charlie Manson

Give me back the Berlin Wall
give me Stalin and St. Paul
Give me Christ
or give me Hiroshima
Destroy another fetus now
We don't like children anyhow
I've seen the future, baby:
it is murder.

Things are going to slide in all directions
Won't be nothing
Nothing you can measure any more
The blizzard of the world
has crossed the threshold
and it has overturned
the order of the soul
When they said REPENT
I wonder what they meant

Leonard Cohen

An epitaph for our generation we've chiseled out:
"Destroy another fetus now
We don't like children anyhow"

All the arguments for abortion reduce to one fact—we don't like children. In a survey from a woman's magazine, the majority of working moms voted that, if again given the choice whether to have children, they definitely would not.

I wouldn't want to be a child today. If parents decide not to kill their fetus, they still make it plain that children hang around as a burden, requiring special arrangements for their care.

In the final analysis, "Love's the only engine of survival." All of man's accumulated wisdom Leonard captures in this succinct epigram. The subject focuses on advancing toward eternal survival, and that engine won't even start unless we repent. Until then, "I've seen the future, brother: it is murder."

Modern man does not feel he has time to communicate with the fragment of God the Father that lives within our minds. We are making sure that our future involves murder.

***

God,

Why do you tolerate us? We brutally murder your son. We murder your children, many not even born. Hatred rules the hearts of evil men, forcing good men into destructive war after destructive war. Give us hope. Help us to not go down as dumb sheep easily slaughtered. Let us fight bravely, and begin to find a cure.

THE LOVE SONG OF J. ALFRED PRUFROCK

Let us go then, you and I,
When the evening is spread out against the sky
Like a patient etherized upon a table;
Let us go, through certain half-deserted streets,
The muttering retreats
Of restless nights in one-night cheap hotels
And sawdust restaurants with oyster shells:
Streets that follow like a tedious argument
Of insidious intent
To lead you to an overwhelming question . . .
Oh, do not ask, "What is it?"
Let us go and make our visit.

In the room the women come and go
Talking of Michelangelo.

The yellow fog that rubs its back upon the windowpanes,
The yellow smoke that rubs its muzzle on the windowpanes
Licked its tongue into the corners of the evening,
Lingered upon the pools that stand in drains,
Let fall upon its back the soot that falls from chimneys,
Slipped by the terrace, made a sudden leap,
And seeing that it was a soft October night,
Curled once about the house, and fell asleep.

And indeed there will be time
For the yellow smoke that slides along the street,
Rubbing its back upon the windowpanes;
There will be time, there will be time
To prepare a face to meet the faces that you meet;
There will be time to murder and create,
And time for all the works and days of hands
That lift and drop a question on your plate;
Time for you and time for me,
And time yet for a hundred indecisions,
And for a hundred visions and revisions,
Before the taking of a toast and tea.

In the room the women come and go
Talking of Michelangelo.

And indeed there will be time
To wonder, "Do I dare?" and, "Do I dare?"
Time to turn back and descend the stair,
With a bald spot in the middle of my hair—
(They will say: "How his hair is growing thin!")
My morning coat, my collar mounting firmly to the chin,
My necktie rich and modest, but asserted by a simple pin—
(They will say: "But how his arms and legs are thin!")
Do I dare
Disturb the universe?
In a minute there is time
For decisions and revisions which a minute will reverse.

For I have known them all already, known them all—
Have known the evenings, mornings, afternoons,
I have measured out my life with coffee spoons;
I know the voices dying with a dying fall
Beneath the music from a farther room.
    So how should I presume?

And I have known the eyes already, known them all—
The eyes that fix you in a formulated phrase,
And when I am formulated, sprawling on a pin,
When I am pinned and wriggling on the wall,
Then how should I begin
To spit out all the butt-ends of my days and ways?
    And how should I presume?

And I have known the arms already, known them all—
Arms that are braceleted and white and bare
(But in the lamplight, downed with light brown hair!)
Is it perfume from a dress
That makes me so digress?
Arms that lie along a table, or wrap about a shawl.
    And should I then presume?
    And how should I begin?

            .   .   .   .   .

Shall I say, I have gone at dusk through narrow streets
And watched the smoke that rises from the pipes
Of lonely men in shirt-sleeves, leaning out of windows? . . .

I should have been a pair of ragged claws
Scuttling across the floors of silent seas.

.   .   .   .   .

And the afternoon, the evening, sleeps so peacefully!
Smoothed by long fingers,
Asleep . . . tired . . . or it malingers,
Stretched on the floor, here beside you and me.
Should I, after tea and cakes and ices,
Have the strength to force the moment to its crisis?
But though I have wept and fasted, wept and prayed,
Though I have seen my head (grown slightly bald) brought in upon a platter,
I am no prophet—and here's no great matter;
I have seen the moment of my greatness flicker,
And I have seen the eternal Footman hold my coat, and snicker,
And in short, I was afraid.

And would it have been worth it, after all,
After the cups, the marmalade, the tea,
Among the porcelain, among some talk of you and me,
Would it have been worth while,
To have bitten off the matter with a smile,
To have squeezed the universe into a ball
To roll it toward some overwhelming question,
To say: "I am Lazarus, come from the dead,
Come back to tell you all, I shall tell you all"—
If one, settling a pillow by her head,
    Should say: "That is not what I meant at all.
    That is not it, at all."

And would it have been worth it, after all,
Would it have been worth while,
After the sunsets and the dooryards and the sprinkled streets,
After the novels, after the teacups, after the skirts that trail along the floor—
And this, and so much more?—
It is impossible to say just what I mean!
But as if a magic lantern threw nerves in patterns on a screen:
Would it have been worth while
If one, settling a pillow or throwing off a shawl,
And turning toward the window, should say:

"That is not it at all,
That is not what I meant, at all."

.   .   .   .   .

No! I am not Prince Hamlet, nor was meant to be;
Am an attendant lord, one that will do
To swell a progress, start a scene or two,
Advise the prince; no doubt, an easy tool,
Deferential, glad to be of use,
Politic, cautious, and meticulous;
Full of high sentence, but a bit obtuse;
At times, indeed, almost ridiculous—
Almost, at times, the Fool.

I grow old . . . I grow old . . .
I shall wear the bottoms of my trousers rolled.

Shall I part my hair behind? Do I dare to eat a peach?
I shall wear white flannel trousers, and walk upon the beach.
I have heard the mermaids singing, each to each.

I do not think that they will sing to me.

I have seen them riding seaward on the waves
Combing the white hair of the waves blown back
When the wind blows the water white and black.

We have lingered in the chambers of the sea
By sea-girls wreathed with seaweed red and brown
Till human voices wake us, and we drown.

T.S. Eliot

With a name like J. Alfred Prufrock, did you really expect a love song?

The atmosphere lingers so dull it almost puts us to sleep. Prufrock hangs about, afraid to act, afraid of not understanding and hence of doing the wrong thing, and afraid of his own eternal destiny. Does he appear before St. Peter at the gates of heaven when he hears snickers?

Even the women methodically come and go, and come and go, as opposed to one who waxes enthusiastic and passionate towards life, like Michelangelo.

One well-known line confesses, "I have measured out my life with coffee spoons." As I linger at work waiting for my next coffee break, I know to whom he addresses this poem!

***

Heavenly Father,

How a poet captures the essence of modern man. Like a photo of the soul, we've become spiritually poor and more afraid. Let us regain our faith, our life, and our confidence in your loving care.

Gregg Tomusko

THE SECOND COMING

Turning and turning in the widening gyre
The falcon cannot hear the falconer;
Things fall apart; the center cannot hold;
Mere anarchy is loosed upon the world,
The blood-dimmed tide is loosed, and everywhere
The ceremony of innocence is drowned;
The best lack all conviction, while the worst
Are full of passionate intensity.

Surely some revelation is at hand;
Surely the Second Coming is at hand.
The Second Coming! Hardly are those words out
When a vast image out of *Spiritus Mundi*
Troubles my sight: somewhere in sands of the desert
A shape with lion body and the head of a man,
A gaze blank and pitiless as the sun,
Is moving its slow thighs, while all about it
Reel shadows of the indignant desert birds.
The darkness drops again; but now I know
That twenty centuries of stony sleep
Were vexed to nightmare by a rocking cradle,
And what rough beast, its hour come round at last,
Slouches towards Bethlehem to be born?

W. B. Yeats

22

The spirit of the earth (*animus mundi*) breeds one who resembles more animal than man. For the "first" child born in Bethlehem, his kingdom was not of this world. The second child belongs here. His heralds instill anarchy and disobedience. The second coming arrives as the antichrist.

***

Lord,

Why does evil grow stronger and good men grow weaker? Is there any way to keep Hitler in a history book, to disband the Hitler Youth, the children carrying rifles instead of toys, their childhood stolen from them, to end horrific propaganda seeping with hate?

Lord, grant us courage and wisdom to defeat evil. Let earth be ruled by a heavenly prince, and not a pitiless beast with a blank gaze.

Gregg Tomusko

THE PILGRIM: CHAPTER 33

See him wasted on the sidewalk in his jacket and his jeans
Wearing yesterday's misfortunes like a smile
Once he had a future full of money, love, and dreams
Which he spent like they was going out of style

And he keeps right on a-changing, for the better or the worse
And searching for a shrine he's never found
Never knowing if believing is a blessing or a curse
Or if the going up is worth the coming down

He's a poet (he's a picker)
He's a prophet (he's a pusher)
He's a pilgrim, and a preacher, and a problem when he's stoned
He's a walking contradiction
Partly truth and partly fiction
Taking every wrong direction on his lonely way back home

He has tasted good and evil in your bedrooms and your bars
And he's traded in tomorrow for today
Running from his devils, Lord, and reaching for the stars
And losing all he loved along the way

But if this world keeps right on turning for the better or the worse
And all he ever gets is older and around
From the rocking of the cradle to the rolling of the hearse
The going up was worth the coming down

He's a poet (he's a picker)
He's a prophet (he's a pusher)
He's a pilgrim, and a preacher, and a problem when he's stoned
He's a walking contradiction
Partly truth and partly fiction
Taking every wrong direction on his lonely way back home

There's a lot of wrong directions on that lonely way back home.

Kris Kristofferson

Kris Kristofferson started writing this song about Chris Gantry and ended up writing it about ten, twenty, and more who used chemicals to experiment with reaching a higher plane and greater artistry, or simply to conquer a feeling of "guilt, pride, and a vague sense of despair." Many highly creative, intelligent, and good hearted brethren became naturally attracted to something associated with experiences of peace and brotherly love, spiritual awareness sometimes found in American Indian ceremonies, and artistic accomplishments like *Kubla Khan* by Samuel Taylor Coleridge.

Kristofferson balanced his charity for his fellow artists with the cold reality of what drugs do to one's life. Kristofferson finds something good in everything. Just to be breathing and experience life, to be given the privilege of being able to search for greater faith, makes life worthwhile.

***

Father,

We all make mistakes. The choices today make it harder to rebound. Many talented people, while searching for something, end up destroyed in the search. I know you see us as we could be, at our full potential. Help us to see this in ourselves, and to see you as the artist of this vision.

Gregg Tomusko

DOVER BEACH

The sea is calm tonight.
The tide is full, the moon lies fair
Upon the straits-on the French coast the light
Gleams and is gone; the cliffs of England stand,
Glimmering and vast, out in the tranquil bay.
Come to the window, sweet is the night air!
Only, from the long line of spray
Where the sea meets the moon-blanched land,
Listen! you hear the grating roar
Of pebbles which the waves draw back, and fling,
At their return, up the high strand,
Begin, and cease, and then again begin,
With tremulous cadence slow, and bring
The eternal note of sadness in.

Sophocles long ago
Heard it on the Aegean, and it brought
Into his mind the turbid ebb and flow
Of human misery; we
Find also in the sound a thought,
Hearing it by this distant northern sea.

The Sea of Faith
Was once, too, at the full, and round earth's shore
Lay like the folds of a bright girdle furled.
But now I only hear
Its melancholy, long, withdrawing roar,
Retreating, to the breath
Of the night wind, down the vast edges drear
And naked shingles of the world.

Ah, love, let us be true
To one another! for the world, which seems
To lie before us like a land of dreams,
So various, so beautiful, so new,
Hath really neither joy, nor love, nor light,
Nor certitude, nor peace, nor help for pain;

Kristofferson and Yeats

And we are here as on a darkling plain
Swept with confused alarms of struggle and flight,
Where ignorant armies clash by night

Matthew Arnold

I forever find it difficult to look out upon the world without sadness gradually coming in like the tide. As attractive as the world seems, compared to faithfulness and having someone to love, it really has little to offer.

***

Heavenly Father,

Our relationships, the love we have for you and each other survives death. The rest serves us as mere scaffolding. Help us to nail down what matters.

Gregg Tomusko

LUCINDA MATLOCK

I went to the dances at Chandlerville,
And played snap-out at Winchester.
One time we changed partners,
Driving home in the moonlight of middle June,
And then I found Davis.
We were married and lived together for seventy years,
Enjoying, working, raising the twelve children,
Eight of whom we lost
Ere I had reached the age of sixty.
I spun, I wove, I kept the house, I nursed the sick,
I made the garden, and for holiday
Rambled over the fields where sang the larks,
And by Spoon River gathering many a shell,
And many a flower and medicinal weed –
Shouting to the wooded hills, singing to the green valleys.
At ninety-six I had lived enough, that is all,
And passed to a sweet repose.
What is this I hear of sorrow and weariness,
Anger, discontent, and drooping hopes?
Degenerate sons and daughters,
Life is too strong for you –
It takes life to love Life.

Edgar Lee Masters

Many of the "gifts" we enjoy we received from our ancestors, whose hard work and sacrifices helped provide us additional opportunities and time to rest. If we listen to our grandparent's stories, their lives were often labor intensive. My grandmother, born in 1900, told us all about the Great Depression.

Those who earn leisure time make profitable use of it. Those who did not earn their leisure often destroy themselves by doing nothing.

A difficult life built strong character into many of our ancestors.

***

Lord,

Help me to face every day with joy. I'm alive, the Father loves me, another day to do his will, to experience situations and prepare myself for heaven. Help me to embrace life and its trials with that strength derived from faith that our ancestors relied on wholly.

Gregg Tomusko

RICHARD CORY

Whenever Richard Cory went down town,
    We people on the pavement looked at him;
He was a gentleman from sole to crown,
    Clean favored, and imperially slim.

And he was always quietly arrayed,
    And he was always human when he talked;
But still he fluttered pulses when he said,
    "Good-morning," and he glittered when he walked.

And he was rich—yes, richer than a king—
    And admirably schooled in every grace:
In fine, we thought that he was everything
    To make us wish that we were in his place.

So on we worked, and waited for the light,
    And went without the meat, and cursed the bread;
And Richard Cory, one calm summer night,
    Went home and put a bullet through his head.

Edward Arlington Robinson

The misguided hope that a rich man cannot be really happy—and it somehow pleases us when he takes his own life—plays out as the commercial and hackneyed retelling of "Richard Cory." But it does not resemble this original poem. Here we find an exemplary person who has worked for his achievements: college, a good job, and clothes to make a good impression.

We never know what a person goes through or what thoughts consume him, and we freeze, shocked, when someone whom we hoped to emulate ends his own life.

***

Lord,

Help me to not judge or be envious. We never really know another person. Some always feel something must be missing in their lives. I pray that you satisfy their longing before they do something desperate.

MINIVER CHEEVY

Miniver Cheevy, child of scorn,
　Grew lean while he assailed the seasons;
He wept that he was ever born,
　And he had reasons.

Miniver loved the days of old
　When swords were bright and steeds were prancing;
The vision of a warrior bold
　Would set him dancing.

Miniver sighed for what was not,
　And dreamed, and rested from his labors;
He dreamed of Thebes and Camelot,
　And Priam's neighbors.

Miniver mourned the ripe renown
　That made so many a name so fragrant;
He mourned Romance, now on the town,
　And Art, a vagrant.

Miniver loved the Medici,
　Albeit he had never seen one;
He would have sinned incessantly
　Could he have been one.

Miniver cursed the commonplace
　And eyed a khaki suit with loathing;
He missed the mediaeval grace
　Of iron clothing.

Miniver scorned the gold he sought,
　But sore annoyed was he without it;
Miniver thought, and thought, and thought,
　And thought about it.

Miniver Cheevy, born too late,
　Scratched his head and kept on thinking;
Miniver coughed, and called it fate,
　And kept on drinking.
　　Edward Arlington Robinson

Perhaps since the Roman Empire fell we've continued in a steady state of decline; everyone remembers "better days" as being at least a decade in the past. I loved Alexandre Dumas' adventures of the three musketeers and Louis L'Amour's *Sacketts* in the old West, although I would not want to live in those times. I do, however, miss the innocence, compunctions, and fun of the 1950s. All this passes, gone forever.

The line that most strikes me reveals, "Miniver scorned the gold he sought, but sore annoyed was he without it." The Spirit of Poverty keels over, so impoverished today as no one cares about money although gathering it reigns as a focal pursuit. A relative of mine impressed upon me that he had no love for material objects, that he really did not need this TV that he was leaning on, and then proceeded to spend the rest of the afternoon watching football games and the evening news!

***

Lord,

Let me not be sore without gold, but help me to find employment so I can earn it. Let me not hypocritically believe possessing money equates to something wrong. Help me to earn enough to be comfortable, and to spend and give wisely.

October 21

9:00

10:00

11:00

12:00

1:00

2:00

3:00

4:00

5:00   *Yeats—6:30*

DINNER RESERVATION: WILLIAM BUTLER YEATS

If, for a large sum, someone asks me to name the greatest poet living or dead, my safest bet would be W. B. Yeats. Chances are that scores as the correct answer.

William grew concerned about the decline of culture, especially among his own Irish. He involved himself in the theater, and in Irish cultural and political movements. His poetry draws from classical symbols to esoteric references, and sometimes simple observations of the natural world. He wants to warn man of his decline, and of the coming of the antichrist. His poetry varies, sometimes extremely straight forward with no interpretation needed, and sometimes quite involved.

William Yeats proved to be his own best critic, which accounts for poetry that almost glows, as from a high quality polish. William has already produced volumes of some of the best poetry ever written in the English language.

His inured approach to life he revealed in lines he asked to be cut on his gravestone, fleeting, ending in a marker not worth stopping to even look at.

His love of beauty and culture through order and elegance he expressed in prayerful wishes to his newborn daughter:

"Ceremony's a name for the rich horn
 And custom for the spreading laurel tree."

William also succeeds as a playwright, ever-infusing new life with a passion into the Irish theatre. He believes his work as poet and playwright earned him the 1923 Nobel Prize in Literature.

If of the mind that being a great poet translates into a golden touch for everything else in life, William's letters dispel that notion. Here goes a fellow traveler with his own struggles, meeting success and failure, and who, incidentally, writes some of the best poetry ever seen.

As one of the masters of English poetry, we easily forget William learned English as a second language.

QUOTES FROM W.B. YEATS

The Yeats Reader, A Portable Compendium of Poetry, Drama, and Prose

I thought it was my business in life to be an artist and a poet, and that there could be no business comparable to that.
pg 297, "XXI, Book I: Four Years, 1887-1891," from *The Trembling of the Veil* (1922), *Autobiographical Writings.*

All my life I have been haunted with the idea that the poet should know all classes of men as one of themselves, that he should combine the greatest possible personal realization with the greatest possible knowledge of the speech and circumstance of the world. Fifteen or twenty years ago I remember longing, with this purpose, to disguise myself as a peasant and wander through the West, and then shipping as a sailor.
pgs 354-355, from "Journal," (Written 1909-30, Published 1972) , 35, *Autobiographical Writings.*

How can the arts overcome the slow dying of men's hearts that we call the progress of the world, and lay their hands upon men's heartstrings again, without becoming the garment of religion as in old times?
pg 381, "The Symbolism of Poetry" (1900), IV, from *Ideas of Good and Evil* (1903), *Critical Writings.*

THE ARTS HAVE FAILED; fewer people are interested in them every generation. The mere business of living, of making money, of amusing oneself, occupies people more and more, and makes them less and less capable of the difficult art of appreciation.
pg 382, "Ireland and the Arts" (1901), from *Ideas of Good and Evil* (1903), *Critical Writings.*

We who care deeply about the arts find ourselves the priesthood of an almost forgotten faith, and we must, I think, if we would win the people again, take upon ourselves the method and the fervour of a priesthood.
pg 382, "Ireland and the Arts" (1901), from *Ideas of Good and Evil* (1903), *Critical Writings.*

The Catholic Church is not the less the Church of the people because the Mass is spoken in Latin, and art is not less the art of the people because it does not always speak in the language they are used to.
pg 385, "Ireland and the Arts" (1901), from *Ideas of Good and Evil* (1903), *Critical Writings*.

An art is always at its greatest when it is most human.
pg 389, "The Reform of the Theatre," from *Samhain* (1903).

No people hate as we do in whom that past is always alive; there are moments when hatred poisons my life and I accuse myself of effeminacy because I have not given it adequate expression.   *(The Irish)*
pg 428, "Essays for the Scribner Edition" (1937), Introduction, II *Subject-Matter*.

The Collected Letters of W.B. Yeats, Volume I, 1865-1895

The very feel of the familiar Sligo earth puts me in good spirits. I should like to live here always . . .
pg 33, "To Katharine Tynan" [13 August 1887].

No fear of Madame Blavatsky drawing me into such matters—she is very much against them and hates Spiritulism vehemently—says mediumship and insanity are the same thing.
pg 164, "To John O'Leary" 7 May [1889].

Yes my beard is off! . . . Madame Blavatsky promised me a bad illness in three months through the loss of all the mesmeric force that collects in a beard–one has gone by. When she sees me, she professes to wonder at my being still on my legs.
pgs 202-203, "To Katharine Tynan" [26 December 1889].

By and by I have had to resign from inner section of Theosophical society because of my first article on Lucifer in Weekly Review. They wanted me to promise to criticise them never again in same fashion. I refused because I looked upon request as undue claim to control right of individual to think as best pleased him.
pg 234, "To John O'Leary" [c. 8] November [1890].

Owing to the Rhymers Club I have a certain amont of influence with reviewers.
pg 255, "To Katharine Tynan" [early July 1891].

Is there, then, no hope for the de-Anglicising of our people? Can we not build up a national tradition, a national literature, which shall be none the less Irish in spirit from being English in language?
pg 338, "To the Editor of United Ireland" 17 December 1892.

I need hardly tell you that your praise of 'The Lake Isle of Innisfree' has given me great pleasure. After all it is the liking or disliking of one's fellow craftsmen, especially of those who have attained the perfect expression one does but grope for, which urges one to work on—else were it best to dream ones dreams in silence.
pg 404, "To Robert Louis Stevenson" 24 October [1894].

If proof were required of the extent to which Dublin is dominated by scholastic— perhaps I should say school room—ideals, Mr Colles gives that proof by finding it "ludicrous" that a young writer like myself should make "an earnest protest" against some of the opinions and methods of an older and better known man of letters. Has Mr Colles forgotten that every literary revolution the world has seen has been made because of the readiness of the young to revolt against what Walt Whitman has called "the endless audacity of elected persons?"
pg 437-438, "To the Editor of the Daily Express (Dublin)" 7 February 1895.

The Collected Letters of W.B. Yeats, Volume II, 1896-1900

Your praise of my work gave me great pleasure as your work is to me the most convincing poetry done by any man among us just now. . . . Your work alone has the quietude of wisdom & I do most firmly believe that all art is dedicated to wisdom & not because it teaches anything but because it reveals divine substances.
pgs 64-65, "To Robert Bridges" 7 December [1896].

My first principle in my work is that poetry must make the land in which we live a holy land as Homer made Greece, the Anciant Indians India & the Hebrew Prophets Judea, if it is to have its full vividness. . . . My second principle, which follows from this first, is that the true foundation of literature is folklore, which was the foundation of Homer & of <more than half> Shakespeare but has not been the foundation of more modern writers.

. . . The third principle is that art is not a criticism of life but a revelation of the realities that are behind life. It has no direct relation with morals. It does not seek to make us see life wisely or sanely or clearly as the moralists believe; but it make[s] us see God & there is no vision that runs to the head & makes the feet unsure like that.

pg 129-130, "To Richard Ashe King" 5 August [1897].

The good Sculptor, poet, painter, or musician pleases other men in the long run because he has first pleased himself, the only person whose taste he really understands.

pgs 491-492, "To the Editor of the United Irishman" [20 January 1900].

The Irish poor hardly think of a mothers death as dividing her very far from their children & I have heard them say that when a mother dies all things often go better with her children for she has gone where she can serve them better than she can here. That may endeed be the very truth.

pgs 529-530, "To Olivia Shakespear" [20 May 1900].

The Collected Letters of W.B. Yeats, Volume III, 1901-1904

My dear Shaw: I write to urge you to come over & see our 'Theatre' this year. You will find all that is stirring in Dublin gathered to geather—& Dublin is full of stir just now—& we will get you to speak, if you will be so good. Come over & help us to stir things up still further.

pg 117, "To George Bernard Shaw" [early] October 1901.

P.S. —I must add a sentence or two to what I have said about the conscience. It is made sensitive and powerful by religion, but its dealings with the complexity of life are regulated by literature. . . . Literature, when it is really literature, does not deal with problems of the hour, but with problems of the soul and the character.

pg 134, "To the Editor of the United Irishman" [7 December 1901].

When I was a boy my father was accustomed to read to me passages of verse that seemed to him and to his friends great poetry, and this very stanza was among them; and now that I have edited Blake, and thought much over every line that he wrote, I cannot think that cry "Did He who made the lamb make thee?" less than a cry out of the heart of all wisdom.

pgs 190-191, "To the Editor of the Times Literary Supplement" [before 27 May 1902].

No art can pass away for ever, till the human nature it once delighted has passed away, and that can hardly be until Michael's trumpet.

pg 197, "To the Editor of the Academy" [7 June 1902].

I am sorry to say I am desperately hard up. I have paid my rent & everything up to date except type writing, but unless Elkin Matthews to whom I have written owes me something I shall get away with difficulty.

pg 202, "To Lady Augusta Gregory" 13 June 1902.

Bernard Shaw talks again of writing a play for us. Certainly it would be a great thing for our Company if he will do us an Irish play.

pg 268, "To Lady Augusta Gregory" 4 December 1902.

Dear Friend: I have written to you little and badly of late I am afraid for the truth is you have had a rival in Nietzsche, that strong enchanter. I have read him so much that I have made my eyes bad again. They were getting well it had seemed. Nietzsche completes Blake & has the same roots—I have not read anything with so much excitement, since I got to love Morris's stories which have the same curious astringent joy.

pg 284, "To Lady Augusta Gregory" 26 December 1902.

. . . —How strange that these lyrical & decorative natures shoul[d] so often be short lived—Beardsly Keats, Shelley & lesser men that one has known, though the world has not.

pg 395, "To Margaret Cunningham" [? c. 10 July 1903].

I am not disappointed by not getting money from the three plays, for I above all people know how many are the expenses, and how few are the profits in an enterprise of the kind. You have helped me enormously in America by performing the plays, of that I am certain.
pg 398, "To John Quinn" 14 July [1903].

I am often driven to speak about things that I would keep silent on were it not that it is necessary in a country like Ireland to be continually asserting one's freedom if one is not to lose it altogether.
pgs 398-399, "To John Quinn" 14 July [1903].

I hope you will come and see me when I get back to London in the autumn, and bring your horoscope about which I feel very curious.
pg 400, "To W.T. Horton" 17 July [1903].

Literature is always personal, always one man's vision of the world, one man's experience, and it can only be popular when men are ready to welcome the visions of others.
pg 440, "To the Editor of the United Irishman" 10 October 1903.

Literature is, to my mind, the great teaching power of the world, the ultimate creator of all values, and it is this, not only in the sacred books whose power everybody acknowledges, but by every movement of imagination in song or story or drama that height of intensity and sincerity has made literature at all. Literature must take the responsibility of its power, and keep all its freedom: it must be like the spirit and like the wind that blows where it listeth, it must claim its right to pierce through every crevice of human nature, and to describe the relation of the soul and the heart to the facts of life and of law, and to describe that relation as it is, not as we would have it be, and in so far as it fails to do this it fails to give us that foundation of understanding and charity for whose lack our moral sense can be but cruelty.
pgs 440-441, "To the Editor of the United Irishman" 10 October 1903.

I have found the reporters much more fateguing than I have ever found lecturing. I had a long struggle with a woman reporter yesterday who wanted to print & probably will a number of indiscreet remarks of mine. Here is an example. "What do you think of Kipling?" "I shall say nothing what ever about Kipling if you please. I will say nothing about any living poet. If he would have the goodness to die I would have plenty to say. Good heavens have you written that down?" "Yes it is the one Irish remark you have made."
pg 467, "To Lady Augusta Gregory" [16 November 1903].

I am very sorry I cannot help you with money. I did my best to get you work as you know, but that is all I can do for you.
pg 657, "To James Joyce" 2 October [1904].

I was disappointed by the first act and a half. The stage Irishman who wasn't an Irishman was very amusing, but then I said to myself 'What the devil did Shaw mean by all this Union of Hearts-like conversation? . . . You have said things in this play which are entirely true about Ireland, things which nobody has ever said before, and these are the very things that are most part of the action. It astonishes me that you should have been so long in London and yet have remembered so much.
pgs 660-661, "To George Bernard Shaw" 5 October [1904].

The Collected Letters of W.B. Yeats, Volume IV, 1905-1907

My dear Gwynn: I am very sorry but I don't like your play. It makes me doubt very much if power as a novelist often goes with dramatic power. You struggle— as it seems to me—to do something which your very talents unfit you for doing. It is all too scattered—the first act is not even essential—It merely tells the audience what they all know & there is little new in the way of telling—your imagination is hampered by an unfamiliar medium. . . Try & forget it is history—say this is a story I have invented & then ask yourself why you invented it. What is the Universal idea it has been made to express.
pgs 141-143, "To Stephen Gwynn" 30 July [1905].

I have altogether re-written my Shadowy Waters. There is hardly a page of the old. The very temper of the thing is different.
pg 179, "To John Quinn" 16 September [1905].

I have often found it a hard thing writing in Ireland to remember clearly at the moment of writing where certain facts have come from—we have no critical press to set the seal of publicity on certain facts & to exclude others.
pg 262, "To Sarah Purser" [30 December 1905].

Please excuse my dictating this, but I have to dictate almost everything because of my eyesight.
pg 267, "To Emery Walker" 31 December 1905.

My lectures were a great success—just like America—the people are more emotional than in England—the Academic people I mean.
pg 316, "To Lady Gregory" [15 January 1906].

I have done apparently very little work for some two or three years, but really a great deal, for I have been rewriting old work stuff to make it fitting for the stage. It is just the kind of work one gets no credit from but learns most from.
pg 398, "To Witter Bynner" 5 May [1906].

The United States have all the old delight in it and have great numbers of people that write stories, and that must be because they are very curious about themselves, and have so much life that has never come into literature. Here in Ireland we are taking to playwriting, because we are curious about ourselves & yet not good readers.
pgs 456-457, "To J. L. Rutledge" 22 July [1906].

The reason I write to you now is that Bernard Shaw tells me that you have a little play about the rebellion of / 98 which might suit the Abbey Theatre, Dublin. He said he thought that our people would be able to play it & that probably another company could not.
pgs 634-635, "TO NORREYS CONNELL" 2 MARCH 1907.

QUOTES FROM W.B. YEATS POEMS

The Collected Poems of W.B. Yeats

I must lie down where all the ladders start
In the foul rag and bone shop of the heart.
—*The Circus Animals' Desertion,* III

Those that I fight I do not hate,
Those that I guard I do not love;
—*An Irish Airman Foresees His Death*

I balanced all, brought all to mind,
The years to come seemed waste of breath,
A waste of breath the years behind
In balance with this life, this death.
—*An Irish Airman Foresees His Death*

Things fall apart; the centre cannot hold;
Mere anarchy is loosed upon the world,
—*The Second Coming*

The best lack all conviction, while the worst
Are full of passionate intensity.
—*The Second Coming*

For men were born to pray and save:
—*September 1913*

Romantic Ireland's dead and gone,
It's with O'Leary in the grave.
—*September 1913*

All changed, changed utterly:
A terrible beauty is born.
—*Easter 1916*

Too long a sacrifice
Can make a stone of the heart.
—*Easter 1916*

I will arise and go now, and go to Innisfree,
—The Lake Isle of Innisfree

I heard the old, old men say,
'All that's beautiful, drifts away
Like the waters.'
—The Old Men Admiring Themselves in the Water

The trees are in their autumn beauty,
The woodland paths are dry,
Under the October twilight the water
Mirrors a still sky;
—The Wild Swans at Coole

When you are old and grey and full of sleep,
And nodding by the fire, take down this book,
And slowly read, and dream of the soft look
Your eyes had once, and of their shadows deep;
—When You Are Old

Murmur, a little sadly, how Love fled
And paced upon the mountains overhead
And hid his face amid a crowd of stars.
—When You Are Old

An intellectual hatred is the worst,
—A Prayer for My Daughter

How but in custom and in ceremony
Are innocence and beauty born?
Ceremony's a name for the rich horn,
And custom for the spreading laurel tree.
—A Prayer for My Daughter

Come away, O human child!
To the waters and the wild
With a faery, hand in hand,
For the world's more full of weeping than you can understand.
—The Stolen Child

I think it better that in times like these
A poet's mouth be silent, for in truth
We have no gift to set a statesman right;
—On Being Asked for a War Poem

THE OLD MEN ADMIRING THEMSELVES IN THE WATER

I heard the old, old men say,
"Everything alters,
And one by one we drop away."
They had hands like claws, and their knees
Were twisted like the old thorn trees
By the waters.
I heard the old, old men say,
"All that's beautiful drifts away
Like the waters."

W.B. Yeats

The physical beauty of our forms, and finally the form itself, passes on and dissolves like something in water. The things we think about when old vary greatly from the thoughts of youth.

***

Lord,

Physical beauty reaps a lot of benefits. Help us improve our looks by working out and perhaps smiling more. Beauty remains important when we are young. When it fades as we age, so lessens its importance.

WHEN YOU ARE OLD

When you are old and gray and full of sleep,
And nodding by the fire, take down this book,
And slowly read, and dream of the soft look
Your eyes had once, and of their shadows deep;

How many loved your moments of glad grace,
And loved your beauty with love false or true,
But one man loved the pilgrim soul in you,
And loved the sorrows of your changing face;

And bending down beside the glowing bars,
Murmur, a little sadly, how Love fled
And paced upon the mountains overhead
And hid his face amid a crowd of stars.

W.B. Yeats

More and more each day I feel "old and gray and full of sleep."

Remembering a lifetime of love, like glowing embers our heart warmly recalls the faithfulness of a spouse, and sad that they have departed.

***

God,
    When did I get old? When did a comfortable chair suddenly mean so much?

As I lose loved ones, please let me feel your nearness and divine love.

THE WILD SWANS AT COOLE

The trees are in their autumn beauty,
The woodland paths are dry,
Under the October twilight the water
Mirrors a still sky;
Upon the brimming water among the stones
Are nine-and-fifty swans.

The nineteenth autumn has come upon me
Since I first made my count;
I saw, before I had well finished,
All suddenly mount
And scatter wheeling in great broken rings
Upon their clamorous wings.

I have looked upon those brilliant creatures,
And now my heart is sore.
All's changed since I, hearing at twilight,
The first time on this shore,
The bell-beat of their wings above my head,
Trod with a lighter tread.

Unwearied still, lover by lover,
They paddle in the cold
Companionable streams or climb the air;
Their hearts have not grown old;
Passion or conquest, wander where they will,
Attend upon them still.

But now they drift on the still water,
Mysterious, beautiful;
Among what rushes will they build,
By what lake's edge or pool
Delight men's eyes when I awake some day
To find they have flown away?

W.B. Yeats

At my favorite time of the year, autumn, I hike through dry leaves in perfect, cool temperatures, and the first four lines of this poem come to mind and describe the exhilarating feeling with a quiet calm, with words as graceful as the movement, and the stillness of swans.

***

Lord,

White swans gliding on a still pond with colorful leaves reflecting on the surface, brings us peace and an appreciation of nature's beauty. Thank you for such serene loveliness suggesting what our eyes have yet to see.

Gregg Tomusko

THE LAKE ISLE OF INNISFREE

I will arise and go now, and go to Innisfree,
And a small cabin build there, of clay and wattles made:
Nine bean-rows will I have there, a hive for the honeybee,
And live alone in the bee-loud glade.

And I shall have some peace there, for peace comes dropping slow,
Dropping from the veils of the morning to where the cricket sings;
There midnight's all a glimmer, and noon a purple glow,
And evening full of the linnet's wings.

I will arise and go now, for always night and day
I hear lake water lapping with low sounds by the shore;
While I stand on the roadway, or on the pavements gray,
I hear it in the deep heart's core.

W.B. Yeats

When my Golden Retriever looks at me with sad eyes, and my Samoyed, all excited, howls and I could use a break, I announce "I *must* arise and go now, and go to Innisfree"—to a local park for a nice walk and a little peace. This I need to do, for the good of myself and my dogs. My son, glad he came once the walk brings my car back in sight, complains when he "has to come." My daughter looks forward to and enjoys the walk as much as I— and the dogs, do.

***

Lord,

In my mind's eye I find myself with nature. It delights me that you enjoyed the same. On a mountainside or in a garden, you communed with your Father. Let me not miss these opportunities to also commune with our Father.

AN IRISH AIRMAN FORESEES HIS DEATH

I know that I shall meet my fate
Somewhere among the clouds above;
Those that I fight I do not hate,
Those that I guard I do not love;
My country is Kiltartan Cross,
My countrymen Kiltartan's poor,
No likely end could bring them loss
Or leave them happier than before.
Nor law, nor duty bade me fight,
Nor public men, nor cheering crowds,
A lonely impulse of delight
Drove to this tumult in the clouds;
I balanced all, brought all to mind,
The years to come seemed waste of breath,
A waste of breath the years behind
In balance with this life, this death.

W.B. Yeats

When life has lost meaning and a person no longer values himself, he may risk his life. Although this man befriended despair, anyone that can see himself in a cold and critical light, to know and state the naked truth, cannot be far from knowing God.

***

Lord,

I hope the significance of my life stands alone and not tied to my job. Except for a paycheck, it equates to a waste of breath. Help me to regain my enthusiasm, and find occasions to make some difference, and most importantly, to follow through with actions when needed.

November

1

All Saints' Day

9:00

10:00

11:00

12:00

1:00

2:00

3:00

4:00

5:00 *7:30 Lecture on saints, social afterward*

THE BATTLE HYMN OF THE REPUBLIC

Mine eyes have seen the glory of the coming of the Lord:
He is trampling out the vintage where the grapes of wrath are stored;
He hath loosed the fateful lightning of his terrible swift sword.
    His truth is marching on.

I have seen him in the watch-fires of a hundred circling camps;
They have builded him an altar in the evening dews and damps;
I can read his righteous sentence by the dim and flaring lamps.
    His day is marching on.

I have read a fiery gospel, writ in burnished rows of steel:
"As ye deal with my contemners, so with you my grace shall deal;
Let the Hero, born of woman, crush the serpent with his heel,
    Since God is marching on."

He has sounded forth the trumpet that shall never call retreat;
He is sifting out the hearts of men before his judgment-seat:
O, be swift, my soul to answer Him! be jubilant my feet!
    Our God is marching on.

In the beauty of the lilies Christ was born across the sea,
With a glory in his bosom that transfigures you and me;
As he died to make men holy, let us die to make men free,
    While God is marching on.

Julia Ward Howe

Here patiently awaits the stirring, marching song to a spiritual victory! Rally the goodness in your heart and enlist.

There burns a love that's growing, that one day will be fanned and enkindle the whole world. His victory guaranteed, inevitable by his sovereignty. Christ poured out his Spirit of Truth at Pentecost, and his spirit will not rest because of the complete love he holds in his heart for mankind. He wants to transfigure you and me.

Julia Ward Howe awoke in the middle of the night, wrote down these words as a marching song for the Union Army, and went back to bed. When she awoke in the morning she had forgotten the words she had written. Her lyrics intended for an army fighting for a just cause. Someday that army will be the sum of men and women in whom Christ reigns victorious in their hearts.

***

"Come Holy Spirit, fill the hearts of thy faithful and enkindle in them the fire of thy love. Send forth thy spirit and thou shalt be created, and thou shalt renew the face of the earth."

Holy Spirit,

Fill our hearts as you filled Julia's heart to write such inspiring words. Maybe truth still marches on. Maybe God marches on. Maybe we'll find hope. Inspire me, O Holy Spirit, so this war for good we win on earth, once and for all.

ABOU BEN ADHEM

Abou Ben Adhem (may his tribe increase!)
Awoke one night from a deep dream of peace,
And saw within the moonlight in his room,
Making it rich, and like a lily in bloom,
An Angel, writing in a book of gold;
Exceeding peace had made Ben Adhem bold,
And to the presence in the room he said,
"What writest thou?" – The Vision raised its head,
And with a look made of all sweet accord,
Answered, "The names of those who love the Lord."
"And is mine one?" said Abou. "Nay, not so,"
Replied the Angel. Abou spoke more low,
But cheerily still, and said, "I pray thee, then,
Write me as one that loves his fellowmen."

The Angel wrote, and vanished. The next night
It came again, with a great wakening light,
And show'd the names whom love of God had bless'd;
And, lo! Ben Adhem's name led all the rest!

James Henry Leigh Hunt

Many who are unable to love a God that they cannot see can be led to a love of God through their fellow man they can see. The test of our love for God rests in the love we have for our fellow man. Jesus spent his entire life in loving service to his brothers and sisters in the flesh.

We do not know all the saints that lived. Abou may have been a saint.

***

Lord,

You are easy to love, divine and all good. My fellow man languishes fallen and tough to love, and so am I. Help me to care about my fellow man, even when all my needs are not met. Let me pray for my enemies. I can do this only because you've asked me to.

I DREAMED I SAW ST. AUGUSTINE

I dreamed I saw St. Augustine,
Alive as you or me,
Tearing through these quarters
In the utmost misery,
With a blanket underneath his arm
And a coat of solid gold,
Searching for the very souls
Whom already have been sold.

"Arise, arise," he cried so loud
In a voice without restraint
"Come out, ye gifted kings and queens
And hear my sad complaint
No martyr is among ye now
Whom you can call your own
So go on your way accordingly
But know you're not alone"

I dreamed I saw St. Augustine
Alive with fiery breath
And I dreamed I was amongst the ones
That put him out to death.
Oh, I awoke in anger
So alone and terrified
I put my fingers against the glass
And bowed my head and cried

Bob Dylan

When we express the desire to have lived when Jesus walked on earth, we imagine ourselves as one of his followers. However, the majority of the people of that time were not sympathetic with Jesus. Many good, religious people agreed with putting him, and later his saints, to death.

***

God,

Bless the saints who followed you to the end, so many murdered as martyrs. Let their lives inspire me. Help me to become like them. Grant me their courage.

November

2

All Souls' Day

9:00

10:00   *Holy Cross Cemetery — Services*

11:00

12:00

1:00

2:00

3:00

4:00

5:00

Gregg Tomusko

THE SPANISH JEW'S TALE
THE LEGEND OF RABBI BEN LEVI

Rabbi Ben Levi, on the Sabbath, read
A volume of the Law, in which it said,
"No man shall look upon my face and live."
And as he read, he prayed that God would give
His faithful servant grace with mortal eye
To look upon His face and yet not die.

Then fell a sudden shadow on the page,
And, lifting up his eyes, grown dim with age,
He saw the Angel of Death before him stand,
Holding a naked sword in his right hand.
Rabbi Ben Levi was a righteous man,
Yet through his veins a chill of terror ran.
With trembling voice he said, "What wilt thou here?"
The Angel answered, "Lo! the time draws near
When thou must die; yet first, by God's decree,
Whate'er thou askest shall be granted thee."
Replied the Rabbi, "Let these living eyes
First look upon my place in Paradise."

Then said the Angel, "Come with me and look."
Rabbi Ben Levi closed the sacred book,
And rising, and uplifting his gray head,
"Give me thy sword," he to the Angel said,
"Lest thou shouldst fall upon me by the way."
The Angel smiled and hastened to obey,
Then led him forth to the Celestial Town,
And set him on the wall, whence, gazing down,
Rabbi Ben Levi, with his living eyes,
Might look upon his place in Paradise.

Then straight into the city of the Lord
The Rabbi leaped with the Death-Angel's sword,
And through the streets there swept a sudden breath
Of something there unknown, which men call death.
Meanwhile, the Angel stayed without, and cried,
"Come back!" To which the Rabbi's voice replied,
"No! in the name of God, whom I adore,
I swear that hence I will depart no more!"

Then all the Angels cried, "O Holy One,
See what the son of Levi here hath done!
The kingdom of Heaven he takes by violence,
And in Thy name refuses to go hence!"
The Lord replied, "My Angels, be not wroth;
Did e'er the son of Levi break his oath?
Let him remain; for he with mortal eye
Shall look upon my face and yet not die."

Beyond the outer wall the Angel of Death
Heard the great voice, and said, with panting breath,
"Give back the sword, and let me go my way."
Whereat the Rabbi paused, and answered, "Nay!
Anguish enough already hath it caused
Among the sons of men." And while he paused
He heard the awful mandate of the Lord
Resounding through the air, "Give back the sword!"

The Rabbi bowed his head in silent prayer,
Then said he to the dreadful Angel, "Swear
No human eye shall look on it again;
But when thou takest away the souls of men,
Thyself unseen, and with an unseen sword,
Thou wilt perform the bidding of the Lord."
The Angel took the sword again, and swore,
And walks on earth unseen forevermore.

Henry Wadsworth Longfellow

When the angel comes to safely escort our souls to the city of the Lord, he arrives unseen. Perhaps there was a time when we saw the angel and his terrible sword, terrible because he summons us to death. As Rabbi Ben Levi's only request when called, he asked to see the face of God and live. By his humble request, and sagacity earned by experience in the world, this clever man found favor with God, probably even made him laugh, and won a gift for all of mankind!

***

Lord,

It's great you have a sense of humor and understand man's mind. Thank you for sharing our humanity with us, so you can fully sympathize, and chuckle.

At death, our guardian angel will see to the safety of our soul. Thank you for giving us angels to aid, encourage, and guide us through this life, and into our life beyond.

LITTLE BOY BLUE

The little toy dog is covered with dust,
    But sturdy and stanch it stands;
And the little toy soldier is red with rust,
    And his musket molds in his hands.
Time was when the little toy dog was new
    And the soldier was passing fair,
And that was the time when our Little Boy Blue
    Kissed them and put them there.

"Now, don't you go till I come," he said,
    "And don't you make any noise!"
So toddling off to his trundle-bed
    He dreamed of the pretty toys.
And as he was dreaming, an angel song
    Awakened our Little Boy Blue -
Oh, the years are many, the years are long,
    But the little toy friends are true.

Ay, faithful to Little Boy Blue they stand,
    Each in the same old place,
Awaiting the touch of a little hand,
    And the smile of a little face.
And they wonder, as waiting these long years through,
    In the dust of that little chair,
What has become of our Little Boy Blue
    Since he kissed them and put them there.

Eugene Field

As if frozen in time, the parents of a dead child preserved their son's room and playthings. The parents figuratively stopped living, much like the empty room and dusty toys, wondering where their little boy has gone and if they will ever see him again.

Perhaps they coined "blue" as an affectionate nickname for their son's favorite color, or because he filled up the room by being such a happy child that they laughingly called him "our little boy blue."

***

Lord,

It comforts us to know that we will meet our children again after this life.

If only we could live long lives to help our children as much as we can. And our children live long lives. I know this longing originates from the Father's plan.

BY THE FIRESIDE
RESIGNATION

There is no flock, however watched and tended,
    But one dead lamb is there!
There is no fireside, howsoe'er defended,
    But has one vacant chair!

The air is full of farewells to the dying,
    And mournings for the dead;
The heart of Rachel, for her children crying,
    Will not be comforted!

Let us be patient! These severe afflictions
    Not from the ground arise,
But oftentimes celestial benedictions
    Assume this dark disguise.

We see but dimly through the mists and vapors;
    Amid these earthly damps
What seem to us but sad, funereal tapers
    May be heaven's distant lamps.

There is no Death! What seems so is transition;
    This life of mortal breath
Is but a suburb of the life elysian,
    Whose portal we call Death.

She is not dead, - the child of our affection, -
    But gone unto that school
Where she no longer needs our poor protection,
    And Christ himself doth rule.

In that great cloister's stillness and seclusion,
    By guardian angels led,
Safe from temptation, safe from sin's pollution,
    She lives, whom we call dead.

Day after day we think what she is doing
    In those bright realms of air;
Year after year, her tender steps pursuing,
    Behold her grown more fair.

Thus do we walk with her, and keep unbroken
　　The bond which nature gives,
Thinking that our remembrance, though unspoken,
　　May reach her where she lives.

Not as a child shall we again behold her;
　　For when with raptures wild
In our embraces we again enfold her,
　　She will not be a child;

But a fair maiden, in her Father's mansion,
　　Clothed with celestial grace;
And beautiful with all the soul's expansion
　　Shall we behold her face.

And though at times impetuous with emotion
　　And anguish long suppressed,
The swelling heart heaves moaning like the ocean,
　　That cannot be at rest, –

We will be patient, and assuage the feeling
　　We may not wholly stay;
By silence sanctifying, not concealing,
　　The grief that must have way.

Henry Wadsworth Longfellow

I can imagine no greater heart tearing than parents burying their child. We desire to die in their place. The very thought of a child passing we disperse from our conscious thoughts, and ask the Father to protect our little ones. The image of a tiny casket remains with me forever, even though I heard it mentioned only once in a conversation I overheard. I turn my head away from the section in the cemetery with small markers and favorite toys. I do not know how parents have lived these many years with the loss of a child in war. The emotions overwhelm, dealt with in the silence of our hearts.

Longfellow wrote in his diary (11/12/1848), "I feel very sad to-day. I miss very much my dear little Fanny. An inappeasable longing to see her comes over me at times, which I can hardly control."

This reflects not a philosopher ruminating on death. This signifies a father who lost his little girl, who longs to see his dear child, Fanny. And through the eye of faith he does see her—loved, happy, and protected. And he shall see her again.

***

Lord,

Even with faith, and knowing that you will resurrect us, death strikes a terrible blow. Mary saw you suffer and die. We share Mary's grief by meditating on the crucifixion. We share Mary's grief when a loved one dies, especially a son or daughter. Jesus, you are our hope; you are our resurrection and our life.

SHE DWELT AMONG THE UNTRODDEN WAYS

She dwelt among the untrodden ways
    Beside the springs of Dove,
A Maid whom there were none to praise
    And very few to love;

A violet by a mossy stone
    Half hidden from the eye!
– Fair as a star, when only one
    Is shining in the sky.

She lived unknown, and few could know
    When Lucy ceased to be;
But she is in her grave, and, oh,
    The difference to me!

William Wordsworth

People little known to the world we view as sometimes special, and their loss prodigious to those who recognize how special they were.

***

Heavenly Father,

We pray for the soul whom no one on earth knew passed, who dies on foreign soil, whose life was cut short, who died alone, who lost to despair, the poor soul who only knew sadness, the soul that holds only a small flicker of faith. Grant them peace.

November   3

9:00

10:00

11:00

12:00

1:00

2:00

3:00

4:00

5:00   *T.S. Eliot*

DINNER RESERVATION: THOMAS STEARNS ELIOT

The conscience, that little voice that speaks in our minds, surfaces audible in the life work of T.S. Eliot. Thomas developed a deep concern for man. Once he realized how many were undone, he began to identify causes. Man turned his back on the church. And what progress resulted? We make waste of the land. There arises no birth or rebirth—we sit spiritually stagnant, unable to regenerate ourselves. Our work perfunctory and dull, our personality etherized. We evade life and fear death. We drift like hollow men.

Thomas encapsulates centuries of man's wisdom in a few select words. Two of his "word pictures" I recall almost daily, and cause me to pause:

"Life you may evade,
 Death you shall not."

   and

"I will show you fear in a handful of dust."

Thomas would find kinship with the Knights of Columbus, who remember "Time Flies" (Tempus Fugit) and to "Remember Death" (Memento Mori). The Knight's strong support of the church fortifies "The Rock." They prevail as a force for good. And as Thomas reminds us, one thing that never changes, however disguised, stands the perpetual struggle of good and evil. (Chorus from "The Rock" I)

Man battles in despair. God lends a hand as the "way, truth, and life." Thomas perfectly describes the reality of despair that weighs on men in the twentieth century, and now into the twenty-first century, after so many wars. He then offers a solution.

"Yet nothing is impossible, nothing,
 To men of faith and conviction." *(Chorus from "The Rock," VIII)*

Thomas mixed studying philosophy at Harvard with his poetry writing. He worked for a bank in England, and now a publishing firm. His recent poems about cats and their unique personalities offer fun recitation ("Old Possum's Book of Practical Cats").

Thomas also excels as an authority on literature. He imparts expertise on the great authors of each century. He provides numerous essays of piercing and insightful critiques. His ability to see into the heart of an artist, the unique gifts and honest analysis of where one falls short, operates akin to a saintly confessor who penitents say can see their souls. His correction and praise of other critiques, often by a professor emeritus who spent a lifetime studying an author, functions akin to an attorney checking the wording for culpability and correctness to assure an honest portrayal of his client.

Thomas knows Greek and Latin, modern languages, the equivalent of a doctorate from Harvard in philosophy, labored until intimate with the greatest works of literature, wrote some of the finest poems ever penned, plus plays, essays, books, and many critiques. He writes, eminently qualified, as a singular spokesperson.

Thomas created a body of literature as big and deep as the Sea of Galilee. He achieved recognition in this world, receiving the Nobel Prize in Literature in 1948, the same year that he was honored by King George VI with the Order of Merit. But Thomas ranks far more than a great artist: he lives as a Christian. He labors as those "fishers of men" who sailed the seas with Jesus. Thomas continues to advance the cause of Christianity. He goes out and preaches the good news to all nations.

Gregg Tomusko

QUOTES FROM T. S. ELIOT

Selected Essays

What every poet starts from is his own emotions.
pg 117, III "Shakespeare and the Stoicism of Seneca" (1927).

It is a test (a positive test, I do not assert that it is always valid negatively) that genuine poetry can communicate before it is understood.
pg. 200, IV "Dante" (1929).

That in good allegory, like Dante's, it is not necessary to understand the meaning first to enjoy the poetry, but that our enjoyment of the poetry makes us want to understand the meaning.
pg. 229, IV "Dante" (1929).

(I dislike the word "generation," which has been a talisman for the last ten years; when I wrote a poem called *The Waste Land* some of the more approving critics said that I had expressed the "disillusionment of a generation," which is nonsense. I may have expressed for them their own illusion of being disillusioned, but that did not form part of my intention.)
pg 324, VI "Thoughts After Lambeth" (1931).

There is no good in making Christianity easy and pleasant; "Youth," or the better part of it, is more likely to come to a difficult religion that to an easy one.
pgs 328- 329, VI "Thoughts After Lambeth" (1931).

The World is trying the experiment of attempting to form a civilized but non-Christian mentality. The experiment will fail; but we must be very patient in awaiting its collapse; meanwhile redeeming the time: so that the Faith may be preserved alive through the dark ages before us; to renew and rebuild civilization, and save the World from suicide.
pg 342, VI "Thoughts After Lambeth" (1931).

A writer like D. H. Lawrence may be in his effect either beneficial or pernicious. I am not sure that I have not had some pernicious influence myself.
pg 351, VI "Religion and Literature" (1935).

We cannot afford to forget that the first–and not one of the least difficult– requirements of either prose or verse is that it should be interesting.
pg 418, VII "Wilkie Collins and Dickens" (1927).

I mean that he knows too many religions and philosophies, has assimilated their spirit too thoroughly (there is probably no one in England or America who understands early Buddhism better than he) to be able to give himself to any. The result is humanism.
pg 428, VII "The Humanism of Irving Babbitt" (1927).

To put the sentiments in order is a later and an immensely difficult task: intellectual freedom is earlier and easier than complete spiritual freedom.
pg. 438, VII "Second Thoughts about Humanism" (1928).

There is a type of mind, and I have a very close sympathy with it, which can only turn to writing, or only produce its best writing, under the pressure of an immediate occasion; and it is this type of mind which I propose to treat as the journalist's. . . . It is not so much that the journalist works on different material from that of other writers, as that he works from a different, no less and often more honourable, motive.
pg 440, VII "Charles Whibley" (1931).

. . . I can only repeat that whenever I have known both the man and the work of any writer of what seemed to me good prose, the printed word has always reminded me of the man speaking.
pg 444, VII "Charles Whibley" (1931).

If education today seems to deteriorate, if it seems to become more and more chaotic and meaningless, it is primarily because we have no settled and satisfactory arrangement of society, and because we have both vague and diverse opinions about the kind of society we want. Education is a subject which cannot be discussed in a void: our questions raise other questions, social, economic, financial, political. And the bearings are on more ultimate problems even than these: to know what we want in education we must know what we want in general, we must derive our theory of education from our philosophy of life. The problem turns out to be a religious problem.
pg 452, VII "Modern Education and the Classics" (1932).

As soon as this precious motive of snobbery evaporates, the zest has gone out of education; if it is not going to mean more money, or more power over others, or a better social position, or at least a steady and respectable job, few people are going to take the trouble to acquire education. For deteriorate it as you may, education is still going to demand a good deal of drudgery.
pg 453, VII "Modern Education and the Classics" (1932).

(Anyone who has taught children even for a few weeks knows that the size of a class makes an immense difference to the amount you can teach. Fifteen is an ideal number; twenty is the maximum; with thirty much less can be done; with more than thirty most teachers' first concern is simply to keep order, and the clever children creep at the pace of the backward.)
pg 454, VII "Modern Education and the Classics" (1932).

No one can become really educated without having pursued some study in which he took no interest–for it is a part of education to *learn to interest ourselves* in subjects for which we have no aptitude.
pg 457, VII "Modern Education and the Classics" (1932).

The universities are too far gone in secularization, they have too long lost any common fundamental assumption as to what education is for, and they are too big.
pg 459, VII "Modern Education and the Classics" (1932).

As the world at large becomes more completely secularized, the need becomes more urgent that professedly Christian people should have a Christian education, which should be an education both for this world and for the life of prayer in this world.
pg 460, VII "Modern Education and the Classics" (1932).

On Poetry and Poets

The trouble of the modern age is not merely the inability to believe certain things about God and man which our forefathers believed, but the inability to *feel* towards God and man as they did. A belief in which you no longer believe is something which to some extent you can still understand; but when religious feeling disappears, the words in which men have struggled to express it become meaningless.
pg 15, "The Social Function of Poetry" [1945], from *On Poetry.*

If you seek for Shakespeare, you will find him only in the characters he created; for the one thing in common between the characters is that no one but Shakespeare could have created any of them. The world of the great poetic dramatist is a world in which the creator is everywhere present, and everywhere hidden.
pg 112, "The Three Voices of Poetry" [1953], from *On Poetry.*

When the poem has been made, something new has happened, something that cannot be wholly explained by *anything that went before*. That, I believe, is what we mean by 'creation'.
pg 124, "The Frontiers of Criticism" [1956], from *On Poetry.*

If in literary criticism, we place all the emphasis upon *understanding,* we are in danger of slipping from understanding to mere explanation. We are in danger even of pursuing criticism as if it was a science, which it never can be. If, on the other hand, we over-emphasize *enjoyment,* we will tend to fall into the subjective and impressionistic, and our enjoyment will profit us no more than mere amusement and pastime.
pg 131, "The Frontiers of Criticism" [1956], from *On Poetry.*

Whatever his conscious motive, it seems clear to me that Virgil desired to affirm the dignity of agricultural labour, and the importance of good cultivation of the soil for the well-being of the state both materially and spiritually.

pg 140-141, "Virgil and the Christian World" [1951], from *On Poets.*

It was the Greeks who taught us the dignity of leisure; it is from them that we in inherit the perception that the highest life is the life of contemplation. But this respect for leisure, with the Greeks, was accompanied by a contempt for the banausic occupations. Virgil perceived that agriculture is fundamental to civilization, and he affirmed the dignity of manual labour.

pg 141, "Virgil and the Christian World" [1951], from *On Poets.*

There was a great deal in the mediaeval world which was not Christian; and practice in the lay world was very different from that of the religious orders at their best: but at least Christianity did establish the principle that action and contemplation, labour and prayer, are both essential to the life of the complete man. It is possible that the insight of Virgil was recognized by monks who read his works in their religious houses.

pg 141, "Virgil and the Christian World" [1951], from *On Poets.*

Notes towards the Definition of Culture

The first important assertion is that no culture has appeared or developed except together with a religion: according to the point of view of the observer, the culture will appear to be the product of the religion, or the religion the product of the culture.

pg 13.

. . . one symptom of the decline of culture in Britain is indifference to the art of preparing food.

pg 26.

Culture may even be described simply as that which makes life worth living.

pg 26.

Now the zealots of world-government seem to me sometimes to assume, unconsciously, that their unity of organization has an absolute value, and that if differences between cultures stand in the way, these must be abolished. . . . a world culture which was simply a *uniform* culture would be no culture at all. We should have a humanity de-humanised. It would be a nightmare.
pgs 61-62.

And, for the most part, it is *inevitable* that we should, when we defend our religion, be defending at the same time our culture, and vice versa: we are obeying the fundamental instinct to preserve our existence.
pg 78.

And without a common faith, all efforts towards drawing nations closer together in culture can produce only an illusion of unity.
pg 83.

An error of the Germany of Hitler was to assume that every other culture than that of Germany was either decadent or barbaric. Let us have an end of such assumptions.
pg 122.

For the health of the culture of Europe two conditions are required: that the culture of each country should be unique, and that the different cultures should recognise their relationship to each other, so that each should be susceptible of influence from the others.
pg 123.

Only a Christian culture could have produced a Voltaire or a Nietzsche. I do not believe that the culture of Europe could survive the complete disappearance of the Christian Faith. And I am convinced of that, not merely because I am a Christian myself, but as a student of social biology. If Christianity goes, the whole of our culture goes. Then you must start painfully again, and you cannot put on a new culture ready made. You must wait for the grass to grow to feed the sheep to give the wool out of which your new coat will be made. You must pass through many centuries of barbarism. We should not live to see the new culture, nor would our great-great-great-grandchildren: and if we did, not one of us would be happy in it.
pg 126.

To our Christian heritage we owe many things besides religious faith. Through it we trace the evolution of our arts, through it we have our conception of Roman Law which has done so much to shape the Western World, through it we have our conceptions of private and public morality. And through it we have our common standards of literature, in the literatures of Greece and Rome. The Western World has its unity in this heritage, in Christianity and in the ancient civilizations of Greece, Rome and Israel, from which, owing to two thousand years of Christianity, we trace our descent.
pgs 126-127.

But we can at least try to save something of those goods of which we are the common trustees: the legacy of Greece, Rome and Israel, and the legacy of Europe throughout the last 2,000 years. In a world which has seen such material devastation as ours, these spiritual possessions are also in imminent peril.
pg 128.

The Idea of a Christian Society

The more highly industrialized the country, the more easily a materialistic philosophy will flourish in it, and the more deadly that philosophy will be. Britain has been highly industrialized longer than any other country. And the tendency of unlimited industrialism is to create bodies of men and women—of all classes—detached from tradition, alienated from religion, and susceptible to mass suggestion: in other words, a mob. And a mob will be no less a mob if it is well fed, well clothed, well housed, and well disciplined.
pg 19, I.

I am concerned with the dangers to the tolerated minority; and in the modern world, it may turn out that the most intolerable thing for Christians is to be tolerated.
pg 21, I.

A nation's system of education is much more important than its system of government; only a proper system of education can unify the active and the contemplative life, action, and speculation, politics and the arts.
 pg 41, II.

In the present ubiquity of ignorance, one cannot but suspect that many who call themselves Christians do not understand what the word means, and that some who would vigorously repudiate Christianity are more Christian than many who maintain it. And perhaps there will always be individuals who, with great creative gifts of value to mankind, and the sensibility which such gifts imply, will yet remain blind, indifferent, or even hostile. That must not disqualify them from exercising the talents they have been given.
 pg 43, II.

If you will not have God (and He is a jealous God) you should pay your respects to Hitler or Stalin.
 pg 64, IV.

September 6th, 1939. The whole of this book, with Preface and Notes, was completed before it was known that we should be at war.
pg 65, IV.

Might one suggest that the kitchen, the children and the church could be considered to have a claim upon the attention of married women? or that no normal married woman would prefer to be a wage-earner if she could help it? What is miserable is a system that makes the dual wage necessary.
pg 70, Notes.

After Strange Gods, A Primer of Modern Heresy

In a society like ours, worm-eaten with Liberalism, the only thing possible for a person with strong convictions is to state a point of view and leave it at that.
pg 12, Preface.

Furthermore, the essential of any important heresy is not simply that it is wrong: it is that it is partly right. . . .   And in the present state of affairs, with the low degree of education to be expected of public and of reviewers, we are more likely to go wrong than right; we must remember too, than an heresy is apt to have a seductive simplicity, to make a direct and persuasive appeal to intellect and emotions, and to be altogether more plausible than the truth.
pgs 25-26.

One can conceive of blasphemy as doing moral harm to feeble or perverse souls; at the same time one must recognize that the modern environment is so unfavourable to faith that it produces fewer and fewer individuals capable of being injured by blasphemy. One would expect, therefore, that (whatever it may have been at other times) blasphemy would be less employed by the Forces of Evil than at any other time in the last two thousand years. Where blasphemy might once have been a sign of spiritual corruption, it might now be taken rather as a symptom that the soul is still alive, or even that it is recovering animation: for the perception of Good and Evil—whatever choice we may make—is the first requisite of spiritual life. We should do well, therefore, to look elsewhere than to the blasphemer, in the traditional sense, for the most fruitful operations of the Evil Spirit today.

pgs 56-57.

What I have been leading up to is the following assertion: that when morals cease to be a matter of tradition and orthodoxy—that is, of the habits of the community formulated, corrected, and elevated by the continuous thought and direction of the Church—and when each man is to elaborate his own, then *personality* becomes a thing of alarming importance.

pg 58.

But most people are only very little alive; and to awaken them to the spiritual is a very great responsibility: it is only when they are so awakened that they are capable of real Good, but that at the same time they become first capable of Evil.

pg 65.

Never has the printing-press been so busy, and never have such varieties of buncombe and false doctrine come from it.

pg 67.

The first requisite usually held up by the promoters of personality is that a man should "be himself"; and this "sincerity" is considered more important than that the self in question should, socially and spiritually, be a good or a bad one. This view of personality is merely an assumption on the part of the modern world, and is no more tenable than several other views which have been held at various times and in several places. The personality thus expressed, the personality which fascinates us in the work of philosophy or art, tends naturally to be the *unregenerate* personality, partly self-deceived and partly irresponsible, and because of its freedom, terribly *limited* by prejudice and self-conceit, capable of much good or great mischief according to the natural goodness or impurity of the man: and we are all, naturally, impure.

pg 68.

QUOTES FROM T. S. ELIOT PLAYS

Murder in the Cathedral (1935)

Destiny waits in the hand of God, shaping the still unshapen:	Part I
Destiny waits in the hand of God, not in the hands of statesmen.	Part I
The last temptation is the greatest treason: To do the right deed for the wrong reason.	Part I
war among men defiles this world,	Part II
In life there is not time to grieve long.	Part II

The Cocktail Party (1949)

Half the harm that is done in this world Is due to people who want to feel important. They don't mean to do harm – but the harm does not interest them. Or they do not see it, or they justify it Because they are absorbed in the endless struggle To think well of themselves.	Act Two
We must always take risks. That is our destiny.	Act Two
Only by acceptance Of the past will you alter its meaning.	Act Three
every moment is a fresh beginning;	Act Three

QUOTES FROM T. S. ELIOT POEMS

April is the cruelest month,
—*The Waste Land*

human kind cannot bear very much reality.
—*Four Quartets,* "Burnt Norton I"
    (also in *Murder in the Cathedral,* Part II.)

For us, there is only the trying. The rest is not our business.
—*Four Quartets,* "East Coker V"

And the end of all our exploring
Will be to arrive where we started
And know the place for the first time.
—*Four Quartets,* "Little Gidding V"

This is the way the world ends
Not with a bang but a whimper.
—*The Hollow Men,* V

    I am moved by fancies that are curled
Around these images, and cling:
The notion of some infinitely gentle
Infinitely suffering thing.
—*Preludes,* IV

Pray for us now and at the hour of our birth.
—*Animula*

The lot of man is ceaseless labour,
Or ceaseless idleness, which is still harder,
—*Choruses from "The Rock,"* I

And the wind shall say: "Here were decent godless people:
Their only monument the asphalt road
And a thousand lost golf balls."
—*Choruses from "The Rock,"* III

Oh my soul, be prepared for the coming of the Stranger,
Be prepared for him who knows how to ask questions.
—*Choruses from "The Rock,"* III

Men have left GOD not for other gods, they say, but for no god;
   and this has never happened before.
—*Choruses from "The Rock,"* VII

Has the Church failed mankind, or has mankind failed the Church?
When the Church is no longer regarded, not even opposed,
 and men have forgotten
All gods except Usury, Lust and Power.
—*Choruses from "The Rock,"* VII

MARINA

Quis hic locus, quae regio, quae mundi plaga?
What place is this, what country, what region of the world?

What seas what shores what gray rocks and what islands
What water lapping the bow
And scent of pine and the woodthrush singing through the fog
What images return
O my daughter.

Those who sharpen the tooth of the dog, meaning
Death
Those who glitter with the glory of the hummingbird, meaning
Death
Those who sit in the sty of contentment, meaning
Death
Those who suffer the ecstasy of the animals, meaning
Death

Are become unsubstantial, reduced by a wind,
A breath of pine, and the woodsong fog
By this grace dissolved in place

What is this face, less clear and clearer
The pulse in the arm, less strong and stronger –
Given or lent? more distant than stars and nearer than the eye

Whispers and small laughter between leaves and hurrying feet
Under sleep, where all the waters meet.

Bowsprit cracked with ice and paint cracked with heat.
I made this, I have forgotten
And remember.
The rigging weak and the canvas rotten
Between one June and another September.
Made this unknowing, half conscious, unknown, my own.
The garboard strake leaks, the seams need calking.
This form, this face, this life
Living to live in a world of time beyond me; let me
Resign my life for this life, my speech for that unspoken,
The awakened, lips parted, the hope, the new ships.

What seas what shores what granite islands towards my timbers
And woodthrush calling through the fog
My daughter.

T. S. Eliot

Like regaining sanity, seeing things clearly as if for the first time, a new consciousness brings excitement from common things and a sharp separation of good from dissolution. How much work yet needs to be completed, and how much we will accomplish!

William Shakespeare named Pericles' daughter Marina in his play *Pericles Prince of Tyre.* She was lost to her father, then, as a young woman, found again.

"What place is this, what country, what region of the world?" Hercules spoke when regaining his sanity in Seneca's play *The Mad Hercules.*

***

Father,

Give me the intensity to find the right way to live, the faith so critical, and clarity of mind. Father, let me be the man who sells everything to procure that one treasure, the kingdom of heaven. Let me be a house well maintained, the seams caulked, the floor swept, and everything prepared for your son to move in.

CHORUS FROM "THE ROCK"

It is hard for those who have never known persecution,
And who have never known a Christian,
To believe these tales of Christian persecution.
It is hard for those who live near a Bank
To doubt the security of their money.
It is hard for those who live near a Police Station
To believe in the triumph of violence.
Do you think that the Faith has conquered the World
And that lions no longer need keepers?
Do you need to be told that whatever has been, can still be?
Do you need to be told that even such modest attainments
As you can boast in the way of polite society
Will hardly survive the Faith to which they owe their significance?
Men! polish your teeth on rising and retiring;
Women! polish your fingernails:
You polish the tooth of the dog and the talon of the cat.
Why should men love the Church? Why should they love her laws?
She tells them of Life and Death, and of all that they would forget.
She is tender where they would be hard, and hard where they like to be soft.
She tells them of Evil and Sin, and other unpleasant facts.
They constantly try to escape
From the darkness outside and within
By dreaming of systems so perfect that no-one will need to be good.
But the man that is will shadow
The man that pretends to be.
And the Son of Man was not crucified once for all,
The blood of the Martyrs not shed once for all,
The lives of the Saints not given once for all:
But the Son of Man is crucified always
And there shall be Martyrs and Saints.
And if blood of Martyrs is to flow on the steps
We must first build the steps;
And if the Temple is to be cast down
We must first build the Temple.

T.S. Eliot

Many values we cannot know unless we "feelingly" experience a "life adventure" where a choice for good arises as a possibility we become aware of and we then choose that good.

Our present life style where we enjoy leisure, entertainment, freedom of worship, freedom of speech, all made possible by the blood of a brother in faith who so valued these things he gave up his life for them. And if they killed him, the usurpers still live.

One viewpoint questions, "How could the Holocaust occur?" Another asks that given the evil in the world, why doesn't it happen more?

This poem sobers us as a reminder of what was, and what could be again. Because we have not personally lived during various events does not make it impossible for them to happen again and again. We cannot stop working for the good while evil subsides when preparing for an assault.

Did the last Christian die upon a cross?

***

Lord,

Countries change from rational to irrational overnight. Germany stood out as a Christian and intelligent nation until swallowed by darkness; Persia, peaceful and cultured, one day became The Islam Nation of Iran, and night descended.

I could be killed tomorrow. Jesus, give me spiritual strength to face such enemies of humanity.

Let mankind rise to the occasion so that the Son of Man no longer offers himself, crucified over and over. Rather, never again.

JOURNEY OF THE MAGI

"A cold coming we had of it,
Just the worst time of the year
For a journey, and such a long journey:
The ways deep and the weather sharp,
The very dead of winter."
And the camels galled, sore-footed, refractory,
Lying down in the melting snow.
There were times we regretted
The summer palaces on slopes, the terraces,
And the silken girls bringing sherbet.
Then the camel men cursing and grumbling
And running away, and wanting their liquor and women,
And the night-fires going out, and the lack of shelters,
And the cities hostile and the towns unfriendly
And the villages dirty and charging high prices:
A hard time we had of it.

At the end we preferred to travel all night,
Sleeping in snatches,
With the voices singing in our ears, saying
That this was all folly.

Then at dawn we came down to a temperate valley,
Wet, below the snow line, smelling of vegetation;
With a running stream and a water mill beating the darkness,
And three trees on the low sky,
And an old white horse galloped away in the meadow.
Then we came to a tavern with vine-leaves over the lintel,
Six hands at an open door dicing for pieces of silver,
And feet kicking the empty wineskins.
But there was no information, and so we continued
And arrived at evening, not a moment too soon
Finding the place; it was (you may say) satisfactory.

All this was a long time ago, I remember,
And I would do it again, but set down
This set down
This: were we led all that way for
Birth or Death? There was a Birth, certainly,
We had evidence and no doubt. I had seen birth and death,
But had thought they were different; this Birth was
Hard and bitter agony for us, like Death, our death.
We returned to our places, these Kingdoms,
But no longer at ease here, in the old dispensation,
With an alien people clutching their gods.
I should be glad of another death.

T.S. Eliot

Entering one kingdom requires leaving another. Death opens the way for new birth, and birth changes one, as some things wither away. The experiences of this Magi in later life must ring true to the one who observed, "He who loves his life will lose it, while he who hates his life will gain eternal life."

***

Heavenly Father,

Meeting Jesus does change us. Many things we were comfortable with now bother us. Anything that keeps us apart from the Lord must be surrendered. Help me to die to myself. Let me face that lonely road to become an individual before Christ.

November **11**

Veterans Day

9:00

10:00

11:00   *City Hall—Mayor's speech, recognition of veterans*

12:00

1:00

2:00

3:00

4:00

5:00

SUCCESS IS COUNTED SWEETEST

Success is counted sweetest
By those who ne'er succeed.
To comprehend a nectar
Requires sorest need.

Not one of all the purple host
Who took the flag to-day
Can tell the definition,
So clear, of victory,

As he, defeated, dying,
On whose forbidden ear
The distant strains of triumph
Break, agonized and clear!

Emily Dickinson

To be denied increases our desire to want something all the more.

Few citizens love peace and long for victory more than those who offer their own lives to serve in a war.

Many Americans fought in battles we lost, or in a war we lost. On Veterans Day we celebrate a civilian's victory made possible by a soldier's defeat. The *least* we can do is to honor these brave and selfless men.

***

Lord,

Let those who have the courage to fight receive all the rewards; not forgotten in a hospital, not four years behind those who did not go, not meet that smug arrogance that thinks that the more intelligent stayed home. Let those who served and serve receive the full measure of the peace they earn for their fellow men.

VIETNAM BLUES

I was on leave at the time just duckin' the fog
Nosin' around like a hungry dog
In that crazy place called Washington D.C.
I saw a crowd of people on the White House lawn
All carry signs about Viet Nam
So I eased on over to see what I could see.
They were a strange lookin' bunch
But I never did understand 'civilian'.

A feller came to me with a list in his hand
Said "We're gatherin' names to send a telegram
Of sympathy." Then he handed me a pen.
I said "I reckon this is going to the children and wives
Of my friends over there who'd given their lives –"
He says "Uh-uh, buddy, this is going to Ho Chi Minh."
I said "Ho Chi Who?" He said "Ho Chi Minh.
People's Leader. North Vietnam."

Well I wasn't real sure that I was hearin' him right
But I thought we'd better move before we got in a fight
Because my eyes were smartin' and my pulse started hittin' a lick.
And I thought about another telegram I'd read
Telling my buddy's wife that her husband was dead
And it wasn't too long 'till I was feeling downright sick.

Another held a sign that said "We Won't Fight"
And I thought to myself "You got that right.
You'd rather let a soldier die instead."
I said "You ever stop to think that every man
Who died there in that far-off land
Was dying so that you won't wake up dead?"
Course he looked at me like I was crazy.
Just another war-monger.

I left that place and went to town
And hit the first bar that I found
To cool myself and pacify my brain.
See I was on orders back to Viet Nam
To a little place, north of Saigon
And I had about an hour to catch my plane.
So all I mean to say is, I don't like dyin' either,
But I care about how I live.

Kris Kristofferson

This true story became somewhat typical. It will confuse historians to comprehend that those whose lives were being defended sided with those who hoped to kill them.

The emotions rise up so strong that Kristofferson still has trouble getting through his lyrics without tears, now more than fifty years later.

***

Lord,

Keep my brain working. Let me see the truth through the intelligent wiles of propaganda and repetition of lies. Let not fear form my thoughts. Let me not be sold on sophistry. Lord, there are men like you who lay down their lives for others. Bless them! Give me the gift of courage, to live as you, Jesus, and these others have lived.

November

28

Thanksgiving

9:00

10:00

11:00

12:00   *Thanksgiving dinner and reflection*

1:00

2:00

3:00

4:00

5:00

Gregg Tomusko

EVANGELINE

This is the forest primeval. The murmuring pines and the hemlocks,
Bearded with moss, and in garments green, indistinct in the twilight,
Stand like Druids of eld, with voices sad and prophetic,
Stand like harpers hoar, with beards that rest on their bosoms.
Loud from its rocky caverns, the deep-voiced neighboring ocean
Speaks, and in accents disconsolate answers the wail of the forest.

Henry Wadsworth Longfellow

THE SONG OF HIAWATHA

Oh the famine and the fever!
Oh the wasting of the famine!
Oh the blasting of the fever!
Oh the wailing of the children!
Oh the anguish of the women!
All the earth was sick and famished;
Hungry was the air around them,
Hungry was the sky above them,
And the hungry stars in heaven
Like the eyes of wolves glared at them!
Into Hiawatha's wigwam
Came two other guests, as silent
As the ghosts were, and as gloomy,
Waited not to be invited,
Did not parley at the doorway,
Sat there without word of welcome
In the seat of Laughing Water;
Looked with haggard eyes and hollow
At the face of Laughing Water.
And the foremost said: "Behold me!
I am Famine, Bukadawin!"
And the other said: "Behold me!
I am Fever, Ahkosewin!"
And the lovely Minnehaha
Shuddered as they looked upon her,
Shuddered at the words they uttered,
Lay down on her bed in silence,

Kristofferson and Yeats

Hid her face, but made no answer;
Lay there trembling, freezing, burning
At the looks they cast upon her,
At the fearful words they uttered.
   Forth into the empty forest
Rushed the maddened Hiawatha;
In his heart was deadly sorrow,
In his face a stony firmness;
On his brow the sweat of anguish
Started, but it froze and fell not.
....

   All day long roved Hiawatha
In that melancholy forest,
Through the shadow of whose thickets,
In the pleasant days of Summer,
Of that ne'er forgotten Summer,
He had brought his young wife homeward
From the land of the Dacotahs;
When the birds sang in the thickets,
And the streamlets laughed and glistened,
And the air was full of fragrance,
And the lovely Laughing Water
Said with voice that did not tremble,
"I will follow you, my husband!"
...

   "Farewell!" said he, "Minnehaha!
Farewell, O my Laughing Water!
All my heart is buried with you,
All my thoughts go onward with you!
Come not back again to labor,
Come not back again to suffer,
Where the Famine and the Fever
Wear the heart and waste the body.
Soon my task will be completed,
Soon your footsteps I shall follow
To the Islands of the Blessed,
To the Kingdom of Ponemah,
To the Land of the Hereafter!"

Henry Wadsworth Longfellow

Gregg Tomusko

THE COURTSHIP OF MILES STANDISH

Then John Alden spake, and related the wondrous adventure,
From beginning to end, minutely, just as it happened;
How he had seen Priscilla, and how he had sped in his courtship,
Only smoothing a little, and softening down her refusal.
But when he came at length to the words Priscilla had spoken,
Words so tender and cruel: "Why don't you speak for yourself, John?"
Up leaped the Captain of Plymouth, and stamped on the floor, till his armor
Clanged on the wall, where it hung, with a sound of sinister omen.
All his pent-up wrath burst forth in a sudden explosion,
E'en as a hand-grenade, that scatters destruction around it.
Wildly he shouted, and loud: "John Alden! you have betrayed me!"
Me, Miles Standish, your friend! have supplanted, defrauded, betrayed me!
One of my ancestors ran his sword through the heart of Wat Tyler;
Who shall prevent me from running my own through the heart of a traitor?
Yours is the greater treason, for yours is a treason to friendship!
You, who lived under my roof, whom I cherished and loved as a brother;
You, who have fed at my board, and drunk at my cup, to whose keeping
I have intrusted my honor, my thoughts the most sacred and secret, -
You too, Brutus! ah woe to the name of friendship hereafter!
Brutus was Caesar's friend, and you were mine, but henceforward
Let there be nothing between us save war, and implacable hatred!"

Henry Wadsworth Longfellow

Much of what we know about America, her first settlers, her native peoples, and her growing into a nation, we learn through the works of Henry Wadsworth Longfellow.

When I watch excellent actors, I sometimes forget that I'm at a theatre and convinced that I'm witnessing an actual event. In the same way Longfellow involves all my senses, so that I feel I am standing in the forest primeval. He involves my mind, so I know intimately what Hiawatha thinks, how he feels when experiencing something and I start to become him. I know Miles Standish enough to figure how he will react to Priscilla's question concerning "his" courting. Longfellow transforms factual history into human history, through the lives of people whom he brings back to life.

Sitting down at Thanksgiving dinner we enjoy a richer experience knowing what these early Americans endured, and yet fervently gave thanks.

***

Lord,

Should I praise the man or his spiritual fruits, or both? Like a magnificent chestnut tree, under which the humble blacksmith labors, whose branches reach up in praise to heaven, whose shade cheers little children at play, whose deep roots appreciates our many different treasures; to this doctorate of letters, Harvard professor, translator, American poet, father, and man of faith, bless you! Henry lived a full life.

Lord, men like Henry Wadsworth Longfellow uplift all men, and give glory to you.

Let my faith show as it did in Longfellow's life and poetry.

And thank you for that great food and the blessing of a family gathering that we so look forward to every Thanksgiving.

December 19

9:00

10:00

11:00

12:00

1:00

2:00

3:00

4:00

5:00   *7:00 pm—Christmas Party—West Highland Party Center*

CHRISTMAS BELLS

I heard the bells on Christmas Day
Their old, familiar carols play,
    And wild and sweet
    The words repeat
Of peace on earth, good-will to men!

And thought how, as the day had come,
The belfries of all Christendom
    Had rolled along
    The unbroken song
Of peace on earth, good-will to men!

Till, ringing, singing on its way,
The world revolved from night to day,
    A voice, a chime,
    A chant sublime
Of peace on earth, good-will to men!

Then from each black, accursed mouth
The cannon thundered in the South,
    And with the sound
    The carols drowned
Of peace on earth, good-will to men!

It was as if an earthquake rent
The hearth-stones of a continent,
    And made forlorn
    The households born
Of peace on earth, good-will to men!

And in despair I bowed my head;
"There is no peace on earth," I said;
    "For hate is strong,
    And mocks the song
Of peace on earth, good-will to men!"

Then pealed the bells more loud and deep:
"God is not dead; nor doth he sleep!
    The Wrong shall fail,
    The Right prevail,
With peace on earth, good-will to men!"

Henry Wadsworth Longfellow

This remains one of my favorite songs of the Christmas season, especially when sung by Ed Ames. Normally, singers include only the first two and last two verses, making the song more universal. Verses four and five refer specifically to the Civil War, and are personal. Longfellow's son Charles ran away to join the First Massachusetts Cavalry, and Longfellow received word that his son was seriously injured, perhaps even dead, in a skirmish near New Hope Church, Virginia, on November 27, 1863. Longfellow wrote this shortly after, in 1864.

When nothing seems hopeful, we find hope, like that derived from the Son of God unexpectedly appearing on earth as a baby, and we can look upon this darkened world and know that some day God's plan will be done here on this planet.

***

Lord,
    Wartime robs man of all that brings good, and we despair. Deep in despair, in the distance we hear your voice in the pealing of the bells: "Evil will cease to exist someday."

Your kingdom continues to grow, built on blocks of love.

Like on Christmas day, let heaven come to earth. Let the Father's will be done on earth as in heaven. Let despair die in the forgotten past.

Kristofferson and Yeats

'little tree'

little tree
little silent Christmas tree
you are so little
you are more like a flower

who found you in the green forest
and were you very sorry to come away?
see   i will comfort you
because you smell so sweetly

i will kiss your cool bark
and hug you safe and tight
just as your mother would,
only don't be afraid

look   the spangles
that sleep all the year in a dark box
dreaming of being taken out and allowed to shine,
the balls the chains red and gold the fluffy threads,

put up your little arms
and i'll give them all to you to hold
every finger shall have its ring
and there won't be a single place dark or unhappy

then when you're quite dressed
you'll stand in the window for everyone to see
and how they'll stare!
oh but you'll be very proud

and my little sister and i will take hands
and looking up at our beautiful tree
we'll dance and sing
"Noel Noel"

E.E. Cummings

I had forgotten the way in which I spoke and how I felt about Christmas when a child until I read this poem. I become a little boy again. Christmas arrives as a magic time, and I feel concern for the feelings of the little Christmas tree.

Surely such little children inhabit the Kingdom of Heaven.

***

Jesus,

Let me prepare for Christmas; examine my motives to make a contrite confession, spend time reading your words, and think about you and your life here on earth. And then will you fill my heart with joy on Christmas day and I'll feel like a little kid again.

THE THREE KINGS

Three Kings came riding from far away,
    Melchior and Gaspar and Baltasar;
Three Wise Men out of the East were they,
And they travelled by night and they slept by day,
    For their guide was a beautiful, wonderful star.

The star was so beautiful, large, and clear,
    That all the other stars of the sky
Became a white mist in the atmosphere,
And by this they knew that the coming was near
    Of the Prince foretold in the prophecy.

Three caskets they bore on their saddle-bows,
    Three caskets of gold with golden keys;
Their robes were of crimson silk with rows
Of bells and pomegranates and furbelows,
    Their turbans like blossoming almond-trees.

And so the Three Kings rode into the West,
    Through the dusk of night, over hill and dell,
And sometimes they nodded with beard on breast,
And sometimes talked, as they paused to rest,
    With the people they met at some wayside well.

"Of the child that is born," said Baltasar,
    "Good people, I pray you, tell us the news;
For we in the East have seen his star,
And have ridden fast, and have ridden far,
    To find and worship the King of the Jews."

And the people answered, "You ask in vain;
    We know of no king but Herod the Great!"
They thought the Wise Men were men insane,
As they spurred their horses across the plain,
    Like riders in haste, and who cannot wait.

And when they came to Jerusalem,
  Herod the Great, who had heard this thing,
Sent for the Wise Men and questioned them;
And said, "Go down unto Bethlehem,
  And bring me tidings of this new king."

So they rode away; and the star stood still,
  The only one in the gray of morn;
Yes, it stopped, - it stood still of its own free will,
Right over Bethlehem on the hill,
  The city of David, where Christ was born.

And the Three Kings rode through the gate and the guard,
  Through the silent street, till their horses turned
And neighed as they entered the great inn-yard;
But the windows were closed, and the doors were barred,
  And only a light in the stable burned.

And cradled there in the scented hay,
  In the air made sweet by the breath of kine,
The little child in the manger lay,
The child, that would be king one day
  Of a kingdom not human but divine.

His mother Mary of Nazareth
  Sat watching beside his place of rest,
Watching the even flow of his breath,
For the joy of life and the terror of death
  Were mingled together in her breast.

They laid their offerings at his feet;
  The gold was their tribute to a King,
The frankincense, with its odor sweet,
Was for the Priest, the Paraclete,
  The myrrh for the body's burying.

And the mother wondered and bowed her head,
    And sat as still as a statue of stone;
Her heart was troubled yet comforted,
Remembering what the Angel had said
    Of an endless reign and of David's throne.

Then the Kings rode out of the city gate,
    With a clatter of hoofs in proud array;
But they went not back to Herod the Great,
For they knew his malice and feared his hate,
    And returned to their homes by another way.

Henry Wadsworth Longfellow

This poem touches us by its simplicity and beauty. It flows so naturally I did not notice it rhymed, let alone the difficult scheme of rhyming three words and two words in each stanza. The story contains details as if unfolding before our eyes and told by a master storyteller, someone wise who understands the meanings behind events, one able to discern what lies in the hearts of men.

***

Heavenly Father,

How wise were the three kings from the east. They grasped the significance of this birth, whilst all others slept. What wondrous gifts, profound in their meaning. How compassionate, that they knew what disturbed Mary's heart and that she found comfort reliving the angel's visit. Being experienced in this world, these wise men were not fooled by Herod's pretense.

Increase in us the spiritual gift of wisdom to see things clearly in a world asleep to spiritual happenings.

Gregg Tomusko

THE GUEST

Yet if His Majesty, our sovereign lord,
  Should of his own accord
  Friendly himself invite,
And say, "I'll be your guest to-morrow night,"
How should we stir ourselves, call and command
All hands to work!" Let no man idle stand!

Set me fine Spanish tables in the hall,
  See they be fitted all;
  Let there be room to eat;
And order taken that there want no meat.
See every sconce and candlestick made bright,
That without tapers they may give a light.

"Look to the presence: are the carpets spread,
  The dazie o'er the head,
  The cushions in the chairs,
And all the candles lighted on the stairs?
Perfume the chambers, and in any case
Let each man give attendance in his place!"

Thus if a king were coming would we do,
  And, 'twere good reason too;
  For 'tis a duteous thing
To show all honour to an earthly king,
And after all our travail and our cost,
So he be pleased, to think no labour lost.

But at the coming of the King of Heaven
  All's set at six and seven:
  We wallow in our sin,
Christ cannot find a chamber in the inn,
We entertain Him always like a stranger,
And, as at first, still lodge Him in a manger.

  Anonymous

Christmas reminds us to prepare generously and luxuriously a proper place for Christ within our hearts.

At Advent, we take time to prepare for the coming of our sovereign Lord. By comparison, "His Majesty, our sovereign lord" seems of little importance.

***

Lord,

It astonished Soren Kierkegaard that we can be in the presence of God any time we wish. He pondered that if a king desired us to be his son-in-law, lacking papers to sign and any proof, rather it must be accepted on faith to make it true, how would we address such a wonderful offer?

Kierkegaard greatly increased my faith. He meditated on your words for hours, year after year. He wrote entire books examining the meaning of "fear and trembling," "the sickness unto death," and other phrases you spoke.

Help me to be more like Kierkegaard, who chose to be single minded: willing only the good.

December

24

Christmas Eve

9:00

10:00

11:00

12:00

1:00

2:00

3:00

4:00

5:00   *Christmas Eve with the children*

A VISIT FROM ST. NICHOLAS

'Twas the night before Christmas, when all through the house
Not a creature was stirring, not even a mouse;
The stockings were hung by the chimney with care,
In hopes that St Nicholas soon would be there;
The children were nestled all snug in their beds,
While visions of sugar-plums danced in their heads;
And mamma in her 'kerchief, and I in my cap,
Had just settled our brains for a long winter's nap,
When out on the lawn there arose such a clatter,
I sprang from the bed to see what was the matter.
Away to the window I flew like a flash,
Tore open the shutters and threw up the sash.
The moon on the breast of the new-fallen snow
Gave the lustre of mid-day to objects below,
When, what to my wondering eyes should appear,
But a miniature sleigh, and eight tiny reindeer,
With a little old driver, so lively and quick,
I knew in a moment it must be St Nick.
More rapid than eagles his coursers they came,
And he whistled, and shouted, and called them by name;
'Now Dasher! now, Dancer! now, Prancer and Vixen!
On, Comet! on, Cupid! on, Donner and Blitzen!
To the top of the porch! to the top of the wall!
Now dash away! dash away! dash away all!'
As dry leaves that before the wild hurricane fly,
When they meet with an obstacle, mount to the sky,
So up to the house-top the coursers they flew,
With the sleigh full of toys, and St Nicholas too.
And then, in a twinkling, I heard on the roof
The prancing and pawing of each little hoof.
As I drew in my head, and was turning around,
Down the chimney St Nicholas came with a bound.
He was dressed all in fur, from his head to his foot,
And his clothes were all tarnished with ashes and soot.
A bundle of toys he had flung on his back,
And he looked like a peddler, just opening his pack.
His eyes – how they twinkled! his dimples how merry!
His cheeks were like roses, his nose like a cherry!
His droll little mouth was drawn up like a bow,
And the beard of his chin was as white as the snow;

The stump of a pipe he held tight in his teeth,
And the smoke it encircled his head like a wreath;
He had a broad face and a little round belly,
That shook when he laughed, like a bowlful of jelly.
He was chubby and plump, a right jolly old elf,
And I laughed when I saw him, in spite of myself;
A wink of his eye and a twist of his head,
Soon gave me to know I had nothing to dread.
He spoke not a word, but went straight to his work,
And filled all the stockings; then turned with a jerk,
And laying his finger aside of his nose,
And giving a nod, up the chimney he rose;
He sprang to his sleigh, to his team gave a whistle,
And away they all flew like the down of a thistle.
But I heard him exclaim, 'ere he drove out of sight,
'Happy Christmas to all, and to all a good-night.'

Clement Clark Moore

Gather round, as Clement Moore once did when he presented his children this Christmas gift, a poem about St. Nicholas and presents! If it wasn't for Clement's vivid descriptions, my favorite being "like a bowlful of jelly," we would not know what Santa really looks like. And if we forget a reindeer's name, or how Santa accomplishes his work, we can look it up here in this marvelous resource.

***

Jesus,

You are the fact; we enjoy the accouterment fiction. As good fiction, Santa Claus comes to life, embodying the spirit of generosity and love given to us at Christmas.

That statue of Santa Claus kneeling next to the baby Jesus in his crib puts things in the proper perspective.

When children find out that Santa is really their parents, they're not too disappointed. That's quite a compliment!

SILENT NIGHT

Silent Night! Holy Night!
All is calm, all is bright.
Round yon virgin mother and child!
Holy Infant so tender and mild,
Sleep in heavenly peace, sleep in heavenly peace.

Silent Night! Holy Night!
Shepherds quake at the sight!
Glories stream from heaven afar,
Heaven'ly hosts sing Alleluia,
Christ the Saviour, is born! Christ the Saviour, is born!

Silent Night! Holy Night!
Son of God, love's pure light;
Radiant beams from Thy holy face,
With the dawn of redeeming grace,
Jesus Lord, at Thy birth, Jesus Lord, at Thy birth.

Joseph Mohr

Every night enters noisy, save one. The peace in one's heart transforms worry into gladness. The beautiful Christmas story of the gospel lovingly retold in music and song brings a heavenly calm to the entire congregation and each family. While singing, I am taken to Jesus' side. I see his loving mother Mary watching over her sleeping son. Under the stars of night, the scene tender as simple shepherds arrive and see heaven come to earth, bringing us gifts. The Father's own Son born, alive and well here among us! His gifts of divine love and redeeming grace stay forever ready for mankind to open.

Father Joseph Mohr wrote the poem "Silent Night" after midnight mass on Christmas Eve 1818. It turned into a magical night, for as he prepared his sermon from the Gospel passage, "And this shall be a sign unto you: you shall find the babe—" a villager interrupted him and requested he journey high into the Austrian Alps to bless a poor and humble mother and her just-born child. In surroundings similar to Jesus' birth, parents summoned him to the bedside. A few hours later, a celebration summoned him to the bedside of the baby born in Bethlehem, at Christmas morning mass. Joseph gave his poem to Franz Gruber, a music teacher who on Christmas day composed the perfect music, as moving and powerful in its simple beauty as the lyrics. Singing "Silent Night" stands out like church bells calling the faithful each Christmas. It remains beloved throughout the Christian World, and known at one time as the "Song from Heaven."

***

Jesus,

What heavenly words and supernal melody to honor heaven here on earth. A song replete with peace and glory praises your holy birth. Let my heart fill with love, like the love that flows through this work wonderfully crafted to adore you.

December   **25**

Christmas Day

9:00   *Christmas Day Mass and celebration*

10:00

11:00

12:00

1:00   *Christmas dinner and exchange of gifts*

2:00

3:00

4:00

5:00

SPANISH LULLABY

The poor Son of Mary,
    Cradle He had none;
His father was a carpenter,
    So he made Him one.

His father made a cradle
    Of wood he had found;
Mary Mother rocked Him,
    And then He slept sound.

You, too, sleep, my baby,
    Never you fear;
Mother is beside you,
    The Son of God is near.

Louis Untermeyer

The human baby Jesus had no consciousness of his divinity. No different, he slept sound when his mother rocked him.

Mary and Joseph stood, unsure of the child's promised destiny. The Jewish scriptures never expected the deliverer to be divine, only a great leader. Mary wished for a victorious General, and Joseph held to a gentle teacher that enlightened minds.

The daily tasks of caring for the baby and of finding and then working wood in order to provide food for the family soon had way, although the supernal events surrounding His birth Mary and Joseph remembered in their hearts forever.

Another human baby we see here comforted by his mother, just as Mary did for Jesus.

In a sense we enjoy two Christmases: the physical birth of Jesus, and at Pentecost when he poured out his spirit upon mankind so that he can always be near to us, if we so desire. We no longer travel to Bethlehem; Jesus comes to us.

***

Jesus,

You knock at our hearts 24/7. Let us stop what we're doing and let you in. Again to feel that comfort our mother gave, loving us no matter what we did.

Gregg Tomusko

A CHRISTMAS CAROL

An angel told Mary
The wonderful word,
And wandering shepherds
Knelt when they heard.

An angel told Joseph
The baby who smiled
Like a star in the twilight
Was God's own child.

Then even the donkey
And cattle awoke
And close to the manger
His praises spoke.

And kings who were wise men
To Bethlehem came
To worship the infant
And say his name.

Now, angels and wise men
And children sing
For the joy that small Jesus
To earth did bring:

Behold the Child given
By heaven above
Rules all of God's creatures
In peace and love!

Harry Behn

With simplicity, the Christmas story is told. The son of God the Father, a divine infinite spirit, becomes man. The Son's vast universe, where peace reigns, and in which we play an important part, He governs by love. How wise to just say his name! What greater joy can be found on earth than for us to share in the faith that Jesus had in God, *our* Father.

***

Heavenly Father,

Thank God you're in charge! Thank God your kingdom operates organized and administered by love.

We feel the peace and joy of your heavenly kingdom on Christmas day. Thank you for this window into eternity.

January

1

New Year's Day

9:00

10:00   *Do nothing!*

11:00

12:00

1:00

2:00

3:00

4:00

5:00

FOREVER YOUNG

May God bless and keep you always,
May your wishes all come true,
May you always do for others
And let others do for you.
May you build a ladder to the stars
And climb on every rung,
May you stay forever young,
Forever young, forever young,
May you stay forever young.

May you grow up to be righteous,
May you grow up to be true,
May you always know the truth
And see the lights surrounding you.
May you always be courageous,
Stand up right and be strong,
May you stay forever young,
Forever young, forever young,
May you stay forever young.

May your hands always be busy,
May your feet always be swift,
May you have a strong foundation
When the winds of changes shift.
May your heart always be joyful,
May your song always be sung,
May you stay forever young,
Forever young, forever young,
May you stay forever young.

Bob Dylan

This brings to mind many good feelings, so full of well-wishes for others that my wife and I chose it for our wedding ceremony. One line rings true of my mother who does so much for us: "May you always do for others." However, she could better accept the complement, "Let others do for you."

***

Heavenly Father,

May this song be my marching orders for the new year. To adopt this attitude helps us stay forever young better than any remedy.

Father, let me possess a more positive outlook, and heartily wish these blessings to others.

WHEN THE SHIP COMES IN

Oh the time will come up
When the winds will stop
And the breeze will cease to be breathin'.
Like the stillness in the wind
'Fore the hurricane begins,
The hour when the ship comes in.

Oh the seas will split
And the ship will hit
And the sands on the shoreline will be shaking.
Then the tide will sound
And the wind will pound
And the morning will be breaking.

Oh the fishes will laugh
As they swim out of the path
And the seagulls they'll be smiling.
And the rocks on the sand
Will proudly stand,
The hour that the ship comes in.

And the words that are used
For to get the ship confused
Will not be understood as they're spoken.
For the chains of the sea
Will have busted in the night
And will be buried at the bottom of the ocean.

A song will lift
As the mainsail shifts
And the boat drifts on to the shoreline.
And the sun will respect
Every face on the deck,
The hour that the ship comes in.

Then the sands will roll
Out a carpet of gold
For your weary toes to be a-touchin'.
And the ship's wise men
Will remind you once again
That the whole wide world is watchin'.

Oh the foes will rise
With the sleep still in their eyes
And they'll jerk from their beds and think they're dreamin'.
But they'll pinch themselves and squeal
And know that it's for real,
The hour when the ship comes in.

Then they'll raise their hands,
Sayin' we'll meet all your demands,
But we'll shout from the bow your days are numbered.
And like Pharaoh's tribe,
They'll be drownded in the tide,
And like Goliath, they'll be conquered.

Bob Dylan

When the ship comes in it will be a better world. We will all be respected. Indeed, no one will attempt to deceive or use us. Words that sound in our best interest when actually not, we will readily discern as a confused message. And these false ones, if they do not change, will one day cease to exist.

Oh, let the ship come in this new year!

***

Lord,

Let lies and sophistry be no more. Let us love the truth and deal honestly with one another. Help us to be models to our children, and never to take advantage of another soul for as long as we live.

January 19

9:00

10:00

11:00

12:00

1:00

2:00

3:00

4:00

5:00   *Longfellow—Dinner at 6:00*

DINNER RESERVATION: HENRY WADSWORTH LONGFELLOW

Henry Wadsworth Longfellow possesses a singleness of purpose. He knew he wanted to be a poet. And he knew he could not survive by producing literature, even great literature. So he worked out a practical plan that would support his main interest and love, poetry.

Henry earned the rare Doctorate of Letters, as one who can speak and read fluently five foreign languages. Henry traveled extensively and lived in various countries to achieve mastery of each language. He teaches modern languages at Harvard, and has translated poetry from Greek, French, Italian, Spanish, German, and other tongues. He convinced his father, a prominent attorney, that literature befits as the right choice for his son.

Henry began happily married, thoroughly enjoying his children. He then faced the loss of a child, and later the loss of his wife in a home fire, a cross he now bears.

His faith helps him through, in happy moments and in defeat. His belief surfaces not as a subtle undertone in his works, but boldly proclaimed. He assumes other people share the same fervor. This assumption must be correct, for his poems become "best sellers" almost immediately after penned.

Henry honors the early Americans, especially Native Indians, more than anyone else I know. How can I grasp their customs, their daily concerns, how they think about things and approach their problems but through the works of Longfellow? He breathes life back into historical intimates as if they were here with us today and telling us what they planned on doing this very morning.

Many of Henry's writings enter our conversations as favorite sayings, articulate thoughts, and sublime ideals. Some resurface reworked and expressed anew in a modern song. The oft-forgotten source leads back to Longfellow. He continues to impact our lives, and although a Harvard professor, he converses as a simple, ordinary man.

QUOTES OF HENRY WADSWORTH LONGFELLOW

Poems and Other Writings

I NEVER think of my native land without a feeling of pride in my national ancestry.
pg 791, "The Literary Spirit of Our Country."

What will be done, may be predicted from what has already been done; and as national talent is gradually developed in the walks of literature, and unfolds itself in greater vigor and richness day after day, a national literature will be formed.
pg 791, "The Literary Spirit of Our Country."

Revolutions in letters are, indeed, the most gradual of all revolutions. A single day may decide the fate of an empire, the event of an hour sweep a throne from the earth, but years must elapse, ere any sensible changes can be introduced in literature.
pg 791, "The Literary Spirit of Our Country."

If climate and natural scenery have a powerful influence in forming the intellectual character of a nation, our country has certainly much to hope from them.
pg 792, "The Literary Spirit of Our Country."

Poetry has been correctly defined the language of the imagination and the passions; and perhaps there is nothing which more awakens the former than the sublime in nature,—and nothing which more influences the latter, than the beautiful.
pg 793, "The Literary Spirit of Our Country."

Few here think of relying upon the exertion of poetic talent for a livelihood, and of making literature the profession of life. The bar or the pulpit claims the greater part of the scholar's existence, and poetry is made its pastime. This is a defect, which the hand of honourable patronage alone can remedy.
pg 794, "The Literary Spirit of Our Country."

Don Quixote thought he could have made beautiful bird-cages and toothpicks if his brain had not been so full of ideas of chivalry. Most people would succeed in small things, if they were not troubled with great ambitions.
pg 796, "Table-Talk."

A torn jacket is soon mended; but hard words bruise the heart of a child.
pg 796, "Table-Talk."

We often excuse our own want of philanthropy by giving the name of fanaticism to the more ardent zeal of others.
pg 796, "Table-Talk."

The Laws of Nature are just, but terrible. There is no weak mercy in them. Cause and consequence are inseparable and inevitable. The elements have no forbearance. The fire burns, the water drowns, the air consumes, the earth buries. And perhaps it would be well for our race if the punishment of crimes against the Laws of Man were as inevitable as the punishment of crimes against the Laws of Nature, —were Man as unerring in his judgments as Nature.
pg 797, "Table-Talk."

I most eagerly aspire after future eminence in literature, my whole soul burns most ardently for it, and every earthly thought centres on it.
 pg 806, "Chronology 1823-25, Letter to his father during his senior year at college."

I have a void in my heart—a constant feeling of sorrow and bereavement, and utter loneliness...
pg 807, "Chronology 1836, Letter on January 10 after his wife Mary's death."

At all times I shall rejoice in the progress of true liberty, and in freedom from slavery of all kinds; but I cannot for a moment think of entering the political arena.
pg 809, "Chronology 1844, To John Greenleaf Wittier, who asks Longfellow to run for Congress, impressed by Longfellow's Poems on Slavery."

It is the redemption of the country. Freedom is triumphant.

pg 812, "Chronology 1860, Journal entry after Lincoln won the presidential election."

Very dark and dreary within me. I am ashamed to lead so useless and listless a life.

pg 813, "Chronology 1863, Journal entry on January 9. Son Charles runs away to join First Massachusetts Cavalry."

The Poetical Works of Longfellow

I kept it some time in manuscript, unwilling to show it to any one, it being a voice from my inmost heart, at a time when I was rallying from depression.

pg 2, "A Psalm Of Life."

I was reading this morning, just after breakfast, the tenth chapter of Mark, in Greek, the last seven verses of which contain the story of blind Bartimeus, and always seemed to me remarkable for their beauty. At once the whole scene presented itself to my mind in lively colors, — the walls of Jericho, the cold wind through the gateway, the ragged, blind beggar, his shrill cry, the tumultuous crowd, the serene Christ, the miracle;

pg 17, "Blind Bartimeus" written to Mr. Ward on November 3, 1841.

Talked with Theophilus Parsons about English hexameters; and 'almost persuaded him to be a Christian.'

pg 71, "Evangeline," from his Diary, 1847, glad about his choice of a metre for this poem.

I feel very sad to-day. I miss very much my dear little Fanny. An inappeasable longing to see her comes over me at times, which I can hardly control.

pg 107, "By the Fireside Resignation," from his Diary under date of November 12, 1848, after the death of his little daughter Fanny.

I have at length hit upon a plan for a poem on the American Indians, which seems to me the right one and the only. It is to weave together their beautiful traditions into a whole. I have hit upon a measure, too, which I think the right and only one for such a theme.

pg 113, "The Song of Hiawatha," from his Diary under date of June 22, 1854.

For my own part, I am delighted to hear the birds again. Spring always reminds me of the *Palingenesis*, or re-creation, of the old alchemists, who believed that form is indestructible and that out of the ashes of a rose the rose itself could be reconstructed, —if they could only discover the great secret of Nature. It is done every spring beneath our windows and before our eyes ; and is always so wonderful and so beautiful !

pg 287, "Palingenesis," from a letter dated March 20, 1859.

I have endeavored to show in it, among other things, that through the darkness and corruption of the Middle Ages ran a bright, deep stream of Faith, strong enough for all the exigencies of life and death.

pg 361, "Christus: A Mystery," from a letter in 1851.

The subject of *The Divine Tragedy* has taken entire possession of me. All day pondering upon and arranging it.

pg 362, "Christus: A Mystery," from his Diary early in January, 1871.

The great art of translating well lies in the power of rendering literally the words of a foreign author while at the same time we preserve the spirit of the original. But how far one of these requisites of a good translation may be sacrificed to the other — how far the translator is at liberty to embellish the original before him, while clothing it in a new language, is a question which has been decided differently by persons of different tastes.

pg 586,"Translations from the Spanish," in preface to book *Coplas de Manrique*, dated Bowdoin College, August 9, 1833.

(poems translated by Longfellow)

The sculptor, when he transfers to the inanimate marble the form and features of a living being, may be said not only to copy, but to translate. ... By sinking the eye deeper, and making the brow more prominent above it, he produces a stronger light and shade, and thus gives to the statue more of the spirit and life of the original than he could have done by an exact copy. So, too, the translator.
pg 586,"Translations from the Spanish," in preface to book *Coplas de Manrique*, dated Bowdoin College, August 9, 1833.

The poem is indeed very beautiful ; and in parts so touching that more than once in translating it I was blinded with tears.
pg 598, "Translations from the Swedish and Danish," from *The Children of the lord's Supper* by Esaias Ttegner, translated in 1841.

I think I shall translate Jasmin's *Blind Girl of Castel Cuille*, —a beautiful poem, unknown to English ears and hearts, but well deserving to be made known.
pg 623, "Translations from the French," from*The Blind Girl of Castel Cuille* by Jacques Jasmin, from his Diary on the 30th of September, 1849.

Gregg Tomusko

QUOTES FROM HENRY WADSWORTH LONGFELLOW POEMS

The Poetical Works of Longfellow

LISTEN my children, and you shall hear
Of the midnight ride of Paul Revere,
—*Paul Revere's Ride*
    from *Tales of a Wayside Inn,* Part First "The Landlord's Tale"

The earth was beautiful as if new-born;
There was that nameless splendor everywhere,
—*The Falcon of Ser Federigo*
    from *Tales of a Wayside Inn,* Part First "The Student's Tale"

"All things come round to him who will but wait."
—*The Falcon of Ser Federigo*
    from *Tales of a Wayside Inn,* Part First "The Student's Tale"

"A town that boasts inhabitants like me
Can have no lack of good society!"
—*The Birds of Killingworth*
    from *Tales of a Wayside Inn,* Part First "The Poet's Tale"

Ships that pass in the night,
—*Elizabeth*
    from *Tales of a Wayside Inn* Part Third "The Theologian's Tale" IV.

"That's what I always say; if you wish a thing to be well done,
You must do it yourself, you must not leave it to others!"
—*The Courtship of Miles Standish,* "II. Love and Friendship"

"Why don't you speak for yourself, John?"   *(Alden)*
—*The Courtship of Miles Standish,* "III. The Lover's Errand"

"Brutus was Caesar's friend, and you were mine, but henceforward
Let there be nothing between us save war, and implacable hatred!"
—*The Courtship of Miles Standish*, "IV. John Alden"

For every guilty deed
  Holds in itself the seed
Of retribution and undying pain.
—*The Masque of Pandora,* "VIII. In the Garden"

Were half the power that fills the world with terror,
   Were half the wealth bestowed on camps and courts,
Given to redeem the human mind from error,
   There were no need of arsenals or forts:
—*The Arsenal at Springfield*

When I remember thou hast given for me
   All that thou hadst, thy life, thy very name,
   And I can give thee nothing in return.
—*A Nameless Grave*

And looks the whole world in the face,
   For he owes not any man.
—*The Village Blacksmith*

   sail on, O Ship of State!
—*The Building of the Ship*

And learn there may be worship without words.
—*My Cathedral*

I SHOT an arrow into the air,
—*The Arrow and the Song*

I HEARD the bells on Christmas Day
—*Christmas Bells*

Then pealed the bells more load and deep:
"God is not dead; nor doth he sleep!
—*Christmas Bells*

Ye that have eyes, yet cannot see,
—*Blind Bartimeus*

Dust thou art, to dust returnest,
   Was not spoken of the soul.
—*A Psalm of Life*

   And our hearts, though stout and brave,
Still, like muffled drums, are beating
   Funeral marches to the grave.
—*A Psalm of Life*

Lives of great men all remind us
   We can make our lives sublime,
—*A Psalm of Life*

The grave itself is but a covered bridge,
Leading from light to light, through a brief darkness!
—*A Covered Bridge at Lucerne*
   Christus: A Mystery, Part II. "The Golden Legend" V.

All silent as a graveyard!
—*John Endicott*
   Christus: A Mystery, Part III. "The New England Tragedies"
   (Act I Scene II)

      Men sometimes, it is said,
Entertain angels unawares.
—*John Endicott*
   Christus: A Mystery, Part III. "The New England Tragedies"
   (Act I, Scene II)

      Thy God shall be my God,
And where thou goest I will go.
—*John Endicott*
   Christus: A Mystery, Part III. "The New England Tragedies"
   (Act III, Scene III)

   the walls have ears!
—*John Endicott*
   Christus: A Mystery, Part III. "The New England Tragedies"
   (Act IV Scene II)

Thus the old tyranny revives again!
. . .
That takes from us all power; we are but puppets,
And can no longer execute our laws.
—*John Endicott*
   Christus: A Mystery, Part III. "The New England Tragedies"
   (Act IV, Scene III)

The Scripture sayeth it,
But speaketh to the Jews; and we are Christians.   *(about Witchcraft)*
—*Giles Corey of the Salem Farms*
  Christus: A Mystery, Part III. "The New England Tragedies"
  (Act III Scene II)

Here is my body; ye may torture it,
But the immortal soul ye cannot crush!
—*Giles Corey of the Salem Farms*
  Christus: A Mystery, Part III. "The New England Tragedies"
  (Act V Scene II)

The people knew not
What manner of man was passing by their doors,
Until he passed no more;
—*Monologue*
  Michael Angelo: A Fragment, Part Second I.

Nay, I know nothing;
Not even my own ignorance,
—*In the Coliseum*
  Michael Angelo: A Fragment, Part Third IV.

The star of the unconquered will,
—*The Light of Stars*

Know how sublime a thing it is
  To suffer and be strong.
—*The Light of Stars*

No one is so accursed by fate,
No one so utterly desolate,
  But some heart, though unknown,
  Responds unto his own.
—*Endymion*

Into each life some rain must fall,
—*The Rainy Day*

To the dry grass and the drier grain
How welcome is the rain!
—*Rain in Summer*

She floats upon the river of his thoughts!
—*The Spanish Student,* (Act II Scene III)

THE day is done,
—*The Day Is Done*

And resembles sorrow only
　As the mist resembles the rain.
—*The Day Is Done*

What seem to us but sad, funereal tapers
　May be heaven's distant lamps.
—*Resignation*　　(loss of his child)

Safe from temptation, safe from sin's pollution,
　She lives, whom we call dead.
—*Resignation*

We will be patient, and assuage the feeling
　We may not wholly stay;
By silence sanctifying, not concealing,
　The grief that must have way.
—*Resignation*

ALL are architects of Fate,
　Working in these walls of Time;
—*The Builders*

Nothing useless is, or low;
　Each thing in its place is best;
And what seems but idle show
　Strengthens and supports the rest.
—*The Builders*

In the elder days of Art,
　Builders wrought with greatest care
Each minute and unseen part;
　For the Gods see everywhere.
—*The Builders*

THIS is the forest primeval.
—*Evangeline: A Tale of Acadie*

Neither locks had they to their doors, nor bars to their windows;
But their dwellings were open as day and the hearts of the owners;
There the richest was poor, and the poorest lived in abundance.
—*Evangeline: A Tale of Acadie,* (Part The First I.)

When she had passed, it seemed like the ceasing of exquisite music.
—*Evangeline: A Tale of Acadie,* (Part The First I.)

Sorrow and silence are strong, and patient endurance is godlike.
—*Evangeline: A Tale of Acadie,* (Part The Second I.)

And, as she looked around, she saw how Death, the consoler,
Laying his hand upon many a heart, had healed it forever.
—*Evangeline: A Tale of Acadie,* (Part The Second V.)

All your strength is in your union,
All your danger is in discord;
Therefore be at peace henceforward,
And as brothers live together.
—*The Song of Hiawatha,* " I. The Peace-Pipe"

By the shores of Gitche Gumee,
By the shining Big-Sea-Water,   *(Lake Superior)*
—*The Song of Hiawatha,* "III. Hiawatha's Childhood"

"As unto the bow the cord is,
So unto the man is woman;
Though she bends him, she obeys him,
Though she draws him, yet she follows;
Useless each without the other!"
—*The Song of Hiawatha,* "X. Hiawatha's Wooing"

OH the long and dreary Winter!
Oh the cold and cruel Winter!
—*The Song of Hiawatha,* "XX. The Famine"

"A boy's will is the wind's will,
And the thoughts of youth are long, long thoughts."
—*My Lost Youth*

For ye are living poems,
—*Children*

A SHADOW

I said unto myself, if I were dead,
>   What would befall these children? What would be
>   Their fate, who now are looking up to me
>   For help and furtherance? Their lives, I said,
Would be a volume wherein I have read
>   But the first chapters, and no longer see
>   To read the rest of their dear history,
>   So full of beauty and so full of dread.
Be comforted; the world is very old,
>   And generations pass, as they have passed,
>   A troop of shadows moving with the sun;
Thousands of times has the old tale been told;
>   The world belongs to those who come the last,
>   They will find hope and strength as we have done.

Henry Wadsworth Longfellow

Parents fear to leave their children when they're too little to fend for themselves. Much depends on fate and luck when children lack the protection and love of both parents. In the prior generation, when children turned eighteen, parents were in their thirties. Today, parents are often in their fifties.

Henry Wadsworth Longfellow transforms fear into faith. He offers a humble and wise description of ourselves as a troop of shadows, moving, whether we realize it or not, with the sun. We have our day on the planet, and then time moves on for the next generation. We are all given the same sun and the same rain. We were able to find hope and strength, and our children will remember that about us and desire to secure the same.

***

Heavenly Father,

Children need their parents, for children have so many needs. Let us live long lives of loving service to our children, to others, and to you, good Father. Help us to emulate your loving care for us, your children, to our children.

Kristofferson and Yeats

THE FIRE OF DRIFT-WOOD
DEVEREUX FARM, NEAR MARBLEHEAD

We sat within the farm-house old,
    Whose windows, looking o'er the bay,
Gave to the sea-breeze damp and cold
    An easy entrance, night and day.

Not far away we saw the port,
    The strange, old-fashioned, silent town,
The lighthouse, the dismantled fort,
    The wooden houses, quaint and brown.

We sat and talked until the night,
    Descending, filled the little room;
Our faces faded from the sight,
    Our voices only broke the gloom.

We spake of many a vanished scene,
    Of what we once had thought and said,
Of what had been, and might have been,
    And who was changed, and who was dead;

And all that fills the hearts of friends,
    When first they feel, with secret pain,
Their lives thenceforth have separate ends,
    And never can be one again;

The first slight swerving of the heart,
    That words are powerless to express,
And leave it still unsaid in part,
    Or say it in too great excess.

The very tones in which we spake
    Had something strange, I could but mark;
The leaves of memory seemed to make
    A mournful rustling in the dark.

Oft died the words upon our lips,
    As suddenly, from out the fire
Built of the wreck of stranded ships,
    The flames would leap and then expire.

And, as their splendor flashed and failed,
   We thought of wrecks upon the main,
Of ships dismasted, that were hailed
   And sent no answer back again.

The windows, rattling in their frames,
   The ocean, roaring up the beach,
The gusty blast, the bickering flames,
   All mingled vaguely in our speech;

Until they made themselves a part
   Of fancies floating through the brain,
The long-lost ventures of the heart,
   That send no answers back again.

O flames that glowed! O hearts that yearned!
   They were indeed too much akin,
The drift-wood fire without that burned,
   The thoughts that burned and glowed within.

Henry Wadsworth Longfellow

Our friends go separate ways, although we were once so close. As a child, loyalty was everything. We shared dreams, aspirations, endless adventures, and good times. But each year change drifts us helplessly apart.

The desire to find a true and lasting friend God placed within us not to torment us, but to be fulfilled. All our friends help us to "enkindle the fire of Thy love" within.

***

Father,

Around many a campfire I sat and watched the orange flames, discussing this or that, whatever entered into our hearts; or content to just sit and stare, respectful of my own and others' reflective thoughts.

How many friends come and go. We long to drop anchor, commit to one and share our life and trials in marriage. What we're really longing for waits deep in our heart, to be permanently united with you in eternal communion, where we have a loyal friend who will love us for life without end.

NATURE

As a fond mother, when the day is o'er,
　　Leads by the hand her little child to bed,
　　Half willing, half reluctant to be led,
　　And leave his broken playthings on the floor,
Still gazing at them through the open door,
　　Nor wholly reassured and comforted
　　By promises of others in their stead,
　　Which, though more splendid, may not please him more;
So Nature deals with us, and takes away
　　Our playthings one by one, and by the hand
　　Leads us to rest so gently, that we go
Scarce knowing if we wish to go or stay,
　　Being too full of sleep to understand
　　How far the unknown transcends the what we know.

Henry Wadsworth Longfellow

What more gentle analogy than our loving mother leading us to bed could the natural occurrence of the end of our lives on earth be compared to?

Perhaps if we knew what awaited us after death, we would more easily relinquish the treasures we own. All we can do is have faith, as a child trusts his mother when she leads him by the hand.

***

Lord,

Old age and death keeps getting closer. Someday it will no longer be "that other guy." Give me the grace to accept my decline, the accompanying pain and loneliness, and to meet death with courage and hope, for you showed us how.

February

14
Valentine's Day

9:00

10:00

11:00

12:00

1:00

2:00

3:00

4:00

5:00   *Dinner Reservations 6:45 — Steak House on Cliff Blvd.*

Gregg Tomusko

UNDER THE OAK

You, if you were sensible,
When I tell you the stars flash signals, each one dreadful,
You would not turn and answer me
"The night is wonderful."

Even you, if you knew
How this darkness soaks me through and through, and infuses
Unholy fear in my essence, you would pause to distinguish
What hurts, from what amuses.

For I tell you
Beneath this powerful tree, my whole soul's fluid
Oozes away from me as a sacrifice steam
At the knife of a Druid.

Again I tell you, I bleed, I am bound with withies,
My life runs out.
I tell you my blood runs out on the floor of this oak,
Gout upon gout.

Above me springs the blood-born mistletoe
In the shady smoke.
But who are you, twittering to and fro
Beneath the oak?

What things better are you, what worse?
What have you to do with the mysteries
Of this ancient place, of my ancient curse?
What place have you in my histories?

D.H. Lawrence

Here we discover a man torn by the intensity of his love.

To D.H. Lawrence, love means recognizing the total "otherness" of a loved one.

***

Lord,

How different God created the two sexes. You made us so that the combination of male and female succeeds unmatched. Although we can never understand each other, we continue to inspire and enjoy each other's company both here and beyond.

LOVING HER WAS EASIER
(Than Anything I'll Ever Do Again)

I have seen the morning burning golden on the mountain in the skies
Aching with the feeling of the freedom of an eagle when she flies
Turning on the world the way she smiled upon my soul as I lay dying
Healing as the colors in the sunshine and the shadows of her eyes

Waking in the morning to the feeling of her fingers on my skin
Wiping out the traces of the people and the places that I've been
Teaching me that yesterday was something that I never thought of trying
Talking of tomorrow and the money, love, and time we had to spend
Loving her was easier than anything I'll ever do again

Coming close together with a feeling that I'd never known before in my time
She ain't ashamed to be a woman or afraid to be a friend
I don't know the answer to the easy way she opened every door in my mind
But dreaming was as easy as believing it was never gonna end
And loving her was easier than anything I'll ever do again

Kris Kristofferson

Love changed this man's life. One who only lived for today found someone authentic, who answered his secret longings. To be attracted to such love comes easy.

***

Lord,

Grace us with a mate who brings us closer to you as we grow closer to each other. In your honor, let us two become as one. Let us give glory to your kingdom by maturing into a family who loves one another.

SUZANNE

Suzanne takes you down
to her place near the river
you can hear the boats go by
you can spend the night beside her
And you know that she's half crazy
but that's why you want to be there
and she feeds you tea and oranges
that come all the way from China
And just when you mean to tell her
that you have no love to give her
she gets you on her wavelength
and she lets the river answer
that you've always been her lover
> *And you want to travel with her*
> *you want to travel blind*
> *and you know that she can trust you*
> *for you've touched her perfect body*
> *with your mind*

And Jesus was a sailor
when he walked upon the water
and he spent a long time watching
from his lonely wooden tower
and when he knew for certain
only drowning men could see him
he said All men will be sailors then
until the sea shall free them
but he himself was broken
long before the sky would open
forsaken, almost human
he sank beneath your wisdom like a stone
> *And you want to travel with him*
> *you want to travel blind*
> *and you think maybe you'll trust him*
> *for he's touched your perfect body*
> *with his mind*

Now Suzanne takes your hand
and she leads you to the river
she is wearing rags and feathers
from Salvation Army counters
And the sun pours down like honey
on our lady of the harbour
And she shows you where to look
among the garbage and the flowers
There are heroes in the seaweed
there are children in the morning
they are leaning out for love
they will lean that way forever
while Suzanne holds the mirror
> *And you want to travel with her*
> *you want to travel blind*
> *and you know that you can trust her*
> *for she's touched your perfect body*
> *with her mind*

Leonard Cohen

I listened to this song in the late sixties, and viewed it as perfect. I feel inspired every time I hear it. If we don't trust a person, we cannot love them. The more someone lives in the truth, the more they mirror the life of Christ. And we want to travel with them. We want to meet them again. We want to be their friend. And we want to travel blind. We don't need elaborate defenses. We can be open and honest and they will never betray that trust. And once we know we can trust them, we will love them. The mind serves as the gateway where the Spirit of Truth enters in, and this Spirit of Jesus makes a person more loving and lovable. The world looks different if viewed from a divine perspective.

An inventive and unique description of the life of Jesus, and the influence of that life upon us, has been rarely attempted or so well accomplished. It remains true that only drowning men make time to see Jesus, and He shows to these few the "heroes in the seaweed" and the "children in the morning."

Incidentally, the one line, "He sank beneath your wisdom like a stone," makes more sense to me as "She sank beneath His wisdom like a stone," if the "He" refers to Jesus, and the "your" to Suzanne.

***

Lord,

To hear a song about Jesus on a commercial album comes around as a rare and wonderful treat. How inspired I am when someone has the courage to talk about your life to a public that wants you silenced. Great men and great poets always discover you, and then want to share their discovery with others.

Gregg Tomusko

TAKE THIS WALTZ
(After Lorca)

Now in Vienna there are ten pretty women.
There's a shoulder where death comes to cry.
There's a lobby with nine hundred windows.
There's a tree where the doves go to die.
There's a piece that was torn from the morning,
And it hangs in the Gallery of Frost –
Ay, ay ay ay
Take this waltz, take this waltz,
take this waltz with the clamp on its jaws.

I want you, I want you, I want you
on a chair with a dead magazine.
In the cave at the tip of the lily,
in some hallway where love's never been.
On a bed where the moon has been sweating,
in a cry filled with footsteps and sand –
Ay, ay ay ay
Take this waltz, take this waltz,
take its broken waist in your hand.

This waltz, this waltz, this waltz, this waltz,
with its very own breath
of brandy and death,
dragging its tail in the sea.

There's a concert hall in Vienna
where your mouth had a thousand reviews.
There's a bar where the boys have stopped talking,
they've been sentenced to death by the blues.
Ah, but who is it climbs to your picture
with a garland of freshly cut tears?
Ay, ay ay ay
Take this waltz, take this waltz,
take this waltz, it's been dying for years.

Kristofferson and Yeats

There's an attic where children are playing,
where I've got to lie down with you soon,
in a dream of Hungarian lanterns,
in the mist of some sweet afternoon.
And I'll see what you've chained to your sorrow,
all your sheep and your lilies of snow –
Ay, ay ay ay
Take this waltz, take this waltz
with its "I'll never forget you, you know!"

And I'll dance with you in Vienna,
I'll be wearing a river's disguise.
The hyacinth wild on my shoulder,
my mouth on the dew of your thighs.
And I'll bury my soul in a scrapbook,
with the photographs there and the moss.
And I'll yield to the flood of your beauty,
my cheap violin and my cross.
And you'll carry me down on your dancing
to the pools that you lift on your wrist –
O my love, o my love
Take this waltz, take this waltz,
it's yours now. It's all that there is.

Leonard Cohen
based on a poem by Federico Garcia Lorca (Little Viennese Waltz)

The intriguing world of a waltz, as seen through the eyes of a poet! "Man does not live by bread alone," and this man, filled with love and truth, understands you cannot live by a waltz alone, either.

When I walked through the Van Gogh Art Museum in Amsterdam, the different images and bold colors inspired me and I left uplifted. Although I didn't understand everything I saw, still the experience demanded my attention and involved me in something wonderful, as dancing a waltz with someone I love, or hearing this song.

***

Heavenly Father,

A beautiful waltz may be all that one has to give. But what a wonderful gift! Like the poor woman who only gave a few mites and sacrificed more than the rest, so this man bequeaths his everything; a magnificent waltz.

February   19

9:00

10:00

11:00

12:00

1:00

2:00

3:00

4:00

5:00   *Kris Kristofferson — 9:00*

DINNER RESERVATION: KRIS KRISTOFFERSON

When I first heard a selection of Kristofferson songs in 1970, I commented, "He combines the beauty of Keats with the truth of (Bob) Dylan!" I endeavored long in the habit of checking who wrote songs that stood out, and Kristofferson kept coming up. So, taking my limited funds, I took a big chance and purchased an entire album, which didn't contain a single song I ever heard. It stands out as the first record where every selection could be called great—not a single bad or "filler" song on it.

Kris Kristofferson served in the army during the Vietnam War, went to Nashville on leave, and fell in love with the singer/songwriter flavor of the city. Johnny Cash greatly impressed him.

As a Rhodes Scholar, he especially loved the works of William Blake. Kris always said he was mostly in it for the writing.

Although he thinks he "sounds like a frog," he records albums, travels the country giving concerts, and enjoys a successful acting career.

He once stated his songs affected "real people." There contains a lot of charity, compassion, and tenderness in his lyrics, as well as naked emotion, sensual love, and an attitude that could be called fundamental, human, and spiritual commingled into one. Kris experienced a wide range of life's experiences and stays willing to share his soul with those who care to listen.

It humbles Kris to tour with his heroes and be on the same stage as Johnny Cash, Willie Nelson, and Waylon Jennings. They call themselves the "Highwaymen," and all four are members of Country Music's Hall of Fame.

As a legend in country music, songwriter, singer, and famous actor, it's hard to believe for two bucks I saw Kris perform on stage at Berea High School, in a small town south of Cleveland.

I see him greatly underappreciated as a writer before and even after Johnny Cash made "Sunday Morning Coming Down" country music's Song of the Year. For over fifty years now when I hear an exceptional song, the author still comes up Kristofferson.

Kris owns a good heart with a deep concern for social justice. He views situations in human terms, still helping the "underdog" that fostered his motive for willing to go to Vietnam, supporting the cause of the migrant worker, or crafting a song about murders in El Salvador, or a sad story in the daily news. His heart guides his pen. He adds compassion to our world.

On June 23, 2011, a veteran of the United States Air Force, country music legend Willie Nelson presented Kris with the Veteran of the Year Award. Kris accepted the award, emotionally moved to tears, and promised to live up to the honor.

***

Each of Kris's songs mirrors a reflection of his soul.

I find the clearest in *Holy Creation*. Like a knight from of old fighting for the truth, replete with acts courageous, bold, and devoid of self-seeking, throughout revealing a tender heart, we watch Kris's soul shine as the lyrics unfold.

Kris owns spiritual credentials of greater worth than his impressive resume. Like in the movie "The Wizard of Oz", where strengths each one believes they lack they actually excel in, so Kris will someday see himself as a wizard of tenderness and humility, aside from being a master wordsmith.

One of Kris's favorites, *Duvalier's Dream* went ignored for several years, lonely as the song's protagonist who stops for whisky to help sort out his affair with someone who loves him.

Few are blessed with as beautiful a voice as Rita Coolidge, and their time together was magical. Rita's album that headlined Kris's (and Carol Pugh's) *The Lady's Not For Sale*, cannot be sung better. The song combines sensitivity and dignity for young woman growing up.

Divorce devastates and we see Kris's heart break for his little girl in *The Last Time* and *Daddy's Song*.

The lost momentum of the early Christian faith along with its forgotten ideals, Kris portrays in *Living Legend*, and earlier in *Breakdown (A Long Way from Home)*.

Kris will probably be most remembered for *Me and Bobby McGee*. The lyrics carry memories of Janis Joplin, the dichotomy of angst against the thrill of freedom as captured by Giulietta Masina in "La Strada", the open road versus the call for comfort found in a home, and that youthful memory of a great time with no regrets.

Seeing a piece of Kris's soul in every song makes each a signature song. If I had my druthers, I'd include the lyrics of all his works. But I've already spent my family's vacation funds!

Gregg Tomusko

SILVER
(THE HUNGER)

Silver was a rounder with a wicked reputation
Music was his magic and his madness rolled in one
It's said he charmed the fairest hearts of this world's fairest maidens
Quick as silver mercury and slippery as a song.

Winding like a river through a thirsty world of strangers
Carving out a legend in a dream-forsaken land
Silver took his pleasures just as freely as he gave them
'Cause hungry eyes weren't quick enough for Silver's flashing hands.

Then once upon escaping from the world of silk and shadows
Sudden growin' sicker of the secrets and the shame
He stumbled onto something real that beckoned like a candle
And never lookin' backwards, he surrendered to the flame.

(Because) Hunger is the surface of a darkened pool of sadness
Silver pale reflection of a deeper need below
Mystery and magic are the holy forms of madness
Sacred as the ecstasy that slumbers in your soul.

Silver moved instinctively within her soft defenses
Soon unfolding mysteries he'd never seen before
And wakening an ancient need, she slipped inside his senses
And Silver took it easy as the closing of a door.

Then soon he touched the secret fears she'd hidden with her sorrows
Darker than her raven hair and deeper than her eyes
And dared to try to lead her to the sunlight from the shadows
Following the line between her laughter and her lies.

But Silver left his magic with the legend he'd abandoned
Love had stripped him naked of illusion and its charms
Then one long night her changing mind took kindly to a stranger
And morning found her moving in the golden stranger's arms.

(Because) Hunger is the surface of a darkened pool of sadness
Silver pale reflection of a deeper need below
Mystery and magic are the holy forms of madness
Sacred as the ecstasy that slumbers in your soul.

Silver stared in silence at the tangled scene before him
Time was burning frozen in the oceans of his eyes
And sadly turning backwards to the world that he'd forsaken
He donned the shining mantle of deception and disguise.

Slowly, with the patience born of silent desperation
Silver worked his way into the darkness of her mind
Weaving through her conscience like a chance she might have taken
Sadder than the shadows of the love she'll never find.

And Silver's spell was stronger than the softly smiling stranger
Whose star was burning smaller in the naked light of day
And Silver took her hand again, a wiser man but sadder
Ready for the strangers who would steal her love away.

(Because) Hunger is the surface of a darkened pool of sadness
Silver pale reflection of a deeper need below
Mystery and magic are the holy forms of madness
Sworn to free the ecstasy that slumbers in your soul.

Kris Kristofferson

I thought this fell into the familiar theme of a playboy who abandoned his ways when finding a woman who loves him for himself. I felt sure Silver would *shun* the shining mantle of deception and disguise. But he donned it; he put it on. This initiates a first, one more true to life.

Many clean-cut, highly ethical men end up puzzled by the choice of a beautiful woman for some unseemly character. What do they see? Music, magic, mystery, and savvy. However, being slick and "with-it" forces one to remain that way to retain his "winnings."

***

Father,

Some men possess a secret magic to attract every sexy woman within sight and then have their pick. That's got to be a blessing! But mystery, without substance, turns superficial, and things fake fade away over time. Lord, let me see my shyness, latest pimple, and limited talent to keep a conversation interesting as a blessing, for it can only attract someone authentic.

SUNDAY MORNIN' COMIN' DOWN

Well I woke up Sunday mornin'
With no way to hold my head that didn't hurt.
And the beer I had for breakfast wasn't bad
So I had one more for dessert.
Then I fumbled through my closet for my clothes
And found my cleanest dirty shirt
And I shaved my face and combed my hair
And stumbled down the stair to meet the day.

I'd smoked my brain the night before
On cigarettes and songs that I'd been pickin'.
But I lit my first and watched a small kid
Cussin' at a can that he was kickin'.
Then I crossed the empty street and caught
The Sunday smell of someone fryin' chicken.
And it took me back to somethin'
That I'd lost somehow, somewhere along the way.

On the Sunday mornin' sidewalks
Wishin' lord that I was stoned
'Cause there's something in a Sunday
Makes a body feel alone.
And there's nothin' short of dyin'
Half as lonesome as the sound
On the sleepin' city sidewalk
Sunday mornin' comin' down.

In the park I saw a daddy
With a laughing little girl who he was swingin'.
And I stopped beside a Sunday school
And listened to the song that they were singin'.
Then I headed back for home
And somewhere far away a lonely bell was ringin'
And it echoed through the canyons
Like the disappearing dreams of yesterday.

On the Sunday mornin' sidewalks
Wishin' lord that I was stoned
'Cause there's something in a Sunday
Makes a body feel alone.
And there's nothin' short of dyin'
Half as lonesome as the sound
On the sleepin' city sidewalk
Sunday mornin' comin' down.

Kris Kristofferson

Sundays seem a little sad, even for a family, because it marks an end to the more relaxed and pleasurable time of a weekend together. Being alone on a Sunday magnifies one's loneliness. Seeing a family at church, enjoying a cookout, and playing with happy children count as blessings not everyone possesses.

***

Lord,

I experienced Sunday mornings coming down. I experienced working the window at McDonalds for minimum wage. I'm lucky to no longer be doing those things.

I don't think anyone wants to face lonely Sundays their whole life. That's why friends leave their drinking buddies for a woman.

I pray for those, for whatever reason, still find themselves doing the same things they did when twenty-one. Give them comfort, embrace them, and remind them in this first life, age twenty-one or one-hundred-and-one you consider "just beginning."

JODY AND THE KID

She would meet me in the morning on my way down to the river
Waiting patient by the chinaberry tree
With her feet already dusty from the pathway to the levee
And her little blue jeans rolled up to her knees
And I'd pay her no attention as she tagged along beside me
Trying hard to copy everything I did
But I couldn't keep from smiling when I'd hear somebody saying
Looky yonder ... there goes Jody and the kid.

Even after we grew older we could still be seen together
As we walked along the levee holding hands
For a surely as the seasons she was changing to a woman
And I'd lived enough to call myself a man
And she often lay beside me in the coolness of the evening
Till the morning sun was shining on my bed
And at times when she was sleeping I would smile when I'd remember
How they used to call us Jody and the kid.

Now the world's a little older and the years have changed the river
'Cause there's houses where there didn't used to be
And on Sundays I go walking down the pathway to the levee
With another little girl who follows me
And it makes the old folks smile to see her tag along beside me
Doing little things the way her mama did
But it gets a little lonesome when I hear somebody saying
Looky yonder ... there goes Jody and the kid.

Kris Kristofferson

Both tender and sad flow these memories. The handful of things we recall in life turn out as sometimes simple, almost silly: to tag along beside me, to copy things I did, to wait for me at the levee; and not so simple: to marry me, and give birth to a little girl, who turned out so much like her mother.

***

Lord,

Give my heart tenderness. Let me appreciate life's simple pleasures, for life passes so quickly.

February 20

9:00

10:00

11:00

12:00

1:00

2:00

3:00

4:00

5:00   *Leonard Cohen —7:30*

DINNER RESERVATION: LEONARD COHEN

As an adolescent, Leonard ran across an old second-hand book of poems by Federico Garcia Lorca, and gladly followed Lorca's verses into a new world of beauty, where Leonard remained ever since. Leonard wrote several novels and books of poetry before he turned to songwriting and singing his own songs. He released several best-selling albums. Many top performers prefer his songs; some doing whole albums of his work. A number of songwriters admire his lyrics and express a hope "to write as well as Leonard."

Leonard's creative juices never stop long enough to congeal. He offers new rhymes, images, and approaches to songs. I'm one of those—whom he suspected of being out there—who cannot wait to listen to his latest song.

Canada teems with pride to claim Leonard as theirs, born in Montreal in 1934. The consulate sponsored a tribute to Leonard and drew many diverse top artists who desired to participate in honoring him. Watching these superb performances, Leonard again got the bug for the stage. Retired, he joked that the idea of performing again becomes more appealing—as we drink! Leonard did just that, and recently completed a world tour that delighted his many loyal fans.

He stopped in the theatre district in downtown Cleveland, Ohio. With many outstanding songs, master musicians, and supernal backup of angelic voices, it is remembered as a special event. Several standing ovations brought him back on stage, disregarding his humorous choices as "It's Closing Time" and "I Tried To Leave You."

I reminisce to forty years ago when Leonard performed at the Smiling Dog Saloon on West 25th Street, in a Cleveland community facing decline. I should also note some of the best entertainers in the nation performed here, and at corner-bar prices. I called it a goldmine.

Since wearing old jeans grew to be a hallmark of the early Seventies, it looked strange to see people standing in line wearing suits in an old Cleveland neighborhood waiting to enter an old bar. Leonard performed song after favorite song till the wee hours. It felt intimate, as if taking place in my living room. He added new verses about "Ships passing in the night" to "Love Calls You by Your Name," which I had never heard before or since. That lone bass lugubriously accompanying Leonard through the morning hours made me love an instrument that I'd never before taken notice of.

Leonard puts his poetry to his music. I'm impressed with someone who can write one great poem. Leonard writes many. He then writes the music and plays it on his guitar. Leonard does not hide the fact that his art takes a lot of work. I respect him for not furthering the popular myth of being born a genius and spinning out songs in a few minutes. Many take a year, and the effort shows.

As Bono remarked, most writers would be happy to use lyrics Leonard discards.

QUOTES OF LEONARD COHEN

The Spice-Box of Earth

Let judges secretly despair of justice: their verdicts will be more acute. Let generals secretly despair of triumph; killing will be defamed. Let priests secretly despair of faith: their compassion will be true.

pg 82," *Lines from My Grandfather's Journal."*

Book of Mercy

To every people the land is given on condition. Perceived or not, there is a Covenant, beyond the constitution, beyond sovereign guarantee, beyond the nation's sweetest dreams of itself.

pg 57, "#27".

Kristofferson and Yeats

QUOTES FROM LEONARD COHEN SONGS

And the steam's coming off her, she's huge and she's shy
And she steps on the moon when she paws at the sky
—*Ballad of the Absent Mare*

Now the flames they followed Joan of Arc
As she came riding through the dark
—*Joan of Arc*

Yes, and thanks for the trouble you took from her eyes.
I thought it was there for good, so I never tried.
—*Famous Blue Raincoat*

I am cold and rainy
—*Queen Victoria and Me*

I feel like an empty cast-iron exhibition
I want ornaments on everything
Because my love she gone with other boys
—*Queen Victoria and Me*

I've heard there was a secret chord
That David played to please the Lord,
But you don't really care for music, do you?
—*Hallelujah*

You loved me as a loser, but now you're worried that I just might win.
You know the way to stop me, but you don't have the discipline.
—*First We Take Manhattan*

They're shutting down the factory now
Just when all the bills are due;
And the fields they're under lock and key
Though the rain and the sun come through.
And springtime starts but then it stops
In the name of something new;
—*Coming Back to You*

You told me again you preferred handsome men,
But for me you would make an exception.
—*Chelsea Hotel*

My friends are gone and my hair is grey.
I ache in the places where I used to play.
—*Tower of Song*

And there's a mighty judgment coming, but I may be wrong.
You see, you hear these funny voices in the tower of song.
—*Tower of Song*

It's coming to America first,
The cradle of the best and of the worst.
It's here they got the range
And the machinery for change
And it's here they got the spiritual thirst.
—*Democracy*

So on battlefields from here to Barcelona
I'm listed with the enemies of love.
—*The Traitor*

It's hard to hold the hand of anyone who's reaching for the sky just to
surrender
—*The Stranger Song*

Sir, I didn't see nothing, I was just getting home late
—*A Singer Must Die*

Many men have loved the bells
You fastened to the rain;
—*Take This Longing*

BIRD ON THE WIRE

Like a bird on the wire
Like a drunk in some midnight choir
I have tried in my way to be free
Like a worm on a hook
Like a knight from some old-fashioned book
I have saved all my ribbons for thee
    If I have been unkind
    I hope that you can just let it go by
    If I have been untrue
    I hope you know it was never to you

Like a baby, stillborn
Like a beast with his horn
I have torn,
Everyone, who reached out for me
But I swear by this song
And by all that I have done wrong
I will make it all up to thee
    I saw a beggar leaning on his wooden crutch
    He said to me "You must not ask for so much"
    And a pretty woman leaning in her darkened door
    She cried to me "Hey, why not ask for more"

Like a bird on the wire
Like a drunk in a midnight choir
I have tried in my way to be free

Leonard Cohen

I always felt that if I could write one good song or poem, I'd have done something really worthwhile in my life. If there was one song I wish I had written, it would be this one. Kris Kristofferson likes it so much he wants the last two lines placed on his tombstone.

I like it so much because every word has personal meaning to me. I've always tried to make my own decisions. And I've hurt people in the process of *my* being free. And I hurt a woman, and others whom I would like to make it up to. And I've faced decisions where both sides seem convincing. And today the job and home ownership and TV eats up so much of my time that there remains little time left. Yet I keep trying, in my own way, to be free.

***

Heavenly Father,

There's the comely girl whom I treated as if unattractive because of my fear of adolescent drives; stayed out all night to prove I'm independent of my worried parents; got drunk to stay close to friends through shared experiences. Thinking I lived free. Lord, I followed along, stupid with no backbone. Please teach me to be an individual by seeking your will and by being totally dependent upon you, for true freedom lies there.

SONG

When with lust I am smitten
To my books I then repair
And read what men have written
Of flesh forbid but fair

But in these saintly stories
Of gleaming thigh and breast
Of sainthood and its glories
Alas I find no rest

For at each body rare
The saintly man disdains
I stare O God I stare
My heart is stained with stains

And casting down the holy tomes
I lead my eyes to where
The naked girls with silver combs
Are combing out their hair

Then each pain my hermits sing
Flies upward like a spark
I live with the mortal ring
Of flesh on flesh in dark

Leonard Cohen

Sex drives through us as a powerful force, and that helps to keep the species going! Being human, the urge sometimes overwhelms, more powerful than the fear of hell, the ingrained lessons of morality, a strong family upbringing, staunch religious practices, or a desire to emulate the lives of the saints.

***

Heavenly Father,

Magazines for men exploit men. Like a mouse trap, casual sex can do serious damage. Tapping into a strong sex drive joining forces with a picturesque imagination, we often surrender to the pleasurable course.

Lord, protect us from near occasions of sin and provide a vision of a loving wife and lighthearted children that transcends brief moments that lessen our self-worth.

ANTHEM

The birds they sang
at the break of day
Start again,
I heard them say,
Don't dwell on what
has passed away
or what is yet to be.

The wars they will
be fought again
The holy dove
be caught again
bought, and sold
and bought again;
the dove is never free.

Ring the bells that still can ring
Forget your perfect offering.
There is a crack in everything.
That's how the light gets in.

We asked for signs
the signs were sent:
the birth betrayed,
the marriage spent;
the widowhood
of every government –
signs for all to see.

Can't run no more
with that lawless crowd
while the killers in high places
say their prayers out loud.
But they've summoned up
a thundercloud
They're going to hear from me.

Ring the bells that still can ring
Forget your perfect offering.
There is a crack in everything.
That's how the light gets in.

You can add up the parts
but you won't have the sum
You can strike up the march,
there is no drum.
Every heart
to love will come
but like a refugee.

Ring the bells that still can ring
Forget your perfect offering.
There is a crack in everything.
That's how the light gets in.

Leonard Cohen

The road to perfection begins with the recognition of our imperfection. We come, all imperfect. Perfect people do not need Jesus, as Leonard observes in *Suzanne* that "Only drowning men could see him" and in this poem:

"There is a crack in everything
That's how the light gets in."

Let's begin on the imperfect road to perfection today.

***

Heavenly Father,

Let us never be so discouraged by our mistakes that we let them distance ourselves from you. The errors of time will be forgotten in eternity.

9:00

10:00

11:00

12:00

1:00

2:00

3:00 *Emily Dickinson—afternoon visit*

4:00

5:00

DINNER RESERVATION: EMILY DICKINSON

I so enjoy the works of Emily that I named my daughter after her, besides finding it a very attractive name. (I differentiate this from Leonard Cohen who named his daughter Lorca, after his favorite poet Federico Garcia Lorca!)

Emily's life can be viewed as unproductive, even wasted. She lives at home and wanders about in the garden, but usually stays inside. Emily does not have a career, and has not raised a family. She never married. As her only hobby, she writes poetry, which is so non-standard the critics consider it trash.

As one picture's explanation may take over a thousand words, so Emily's compact verse says more than other more prolix poems. If we distill the best qualities out of classic novels, we are left with pure Emily Dickinson. Her reader's-digest versions of poetry arrive succinct, meaningful, and a pleasure to read.

Comparing poetry to jewelry, I see Emily's verses as necklaces. Her format contains dashes between capitalized words that actually appear like a necklace: The Bobolink — the Sea —Thunder — the Cricket —Nay — Nature is Harmony — ("Nature" is what we see). Her pearls, some perfect, she strings together in a unique and charming pattern. She capitalizes words much as a musician will accentuate certain notes. Most collections remove her dashes and capitalizations, but some retain the way she wants them to look.

As some women center their lives around someone they hope to be their future husband, so Emily focuses her life round her poems. Most of what she conveys in conversation, she already etched in a poem. The best way to know Emily begins by reading her poems.

Emily found a kinship with her sister-in-law Susan, born nine days apart, Emily on December 10, 1830, and Susan December 19, 1830. They became neighbors who correspond frequently. Emily shared many drafts of her poems with Susan, and surprisingly, or not surprisingly, Emily's letters began to take the shape of her poems. Here are some letters.

LETTERS OF EMILY DICKINSON

Open Me Carefully, Emily Dickinson's Intimate Letters to Susan Huntington Dickinson

I regret to inform you that at 3. oclock yesterday, my mind came to a stand, and has since then been stationary.

. . .

We were much afflicted yesterday, by the supposed removal of <u>our Cat</u> from time to Eternity.

She returned, however, last evening, having been detained by the storm, beyond her expectations.

pgs 37-38, early December, 1852.

<u>Write! Comrade – write!</u>
On this wondrous sea
Sailing silently,
Ho! Pilot, ho!
pg 44, March 1853.

There <u>are</u> lives, sometimes, Susie – Bless God that we catch faint glimpses of his brighter Paradise from <u>occasional</u> Heavens <u>here</u>!
pg 46, March 12, 1853.

I could fill a chamber with landscapes so lone, men should pause and weep there; then haste grateful home, for a loved one left.
pg 51, November 27 to December 3, 1854.

– If I do not come with feet, in my heart I come – talk the most, and laugh the longest – stay when all the rest have gone –
pg 73, late 1850s.

Dear Sue –
   I could
send you no
Note so sweet
as the last
words of
your Boy –
"You will look
after Mother"?
   Emily '
pg 260, summer 1885.

QUOTES FROM EMILY DICKINSON POEMS
Note: Emily did not title any of her poems. Most publishers use the first line.

Parting is all we know of heaven,
   And all we need of hell.
—*My life closed twice before its close* also named *Parting*

I never spoke with God,
Nor visited in Heaven;
Yet certain am I of the spot
As if the chart were given.
—*I never saw a moor* or *Chartless*

He questioned softly why I failed?
"For beauty," I replied.
"And I for truth,–the two are one;
We brethren are," he said.
—*I died for beauty*

But never met this fellow,
Attended or alone,
Without a tighter breathing,
And zero at the bone.
—*A narrow fellow in the grass* or *The Snake*

Because I could not stop for Death,
He kindly stopped for me;
—*Because I could not stop for death* or *The Chariot*

Success is counted sweetest
By those who ne'er succeed.
—*Success is counted sweetest*

Hope is the thing with feathers
That perches in the soul,
—*Hope is a thing with feathers*

I'm nobody! Who are you?
Are you nobody, too?
—*I'm nobody*

This is my letter to the world,
    That never wrote to me,
—*This is my letter to the world*

Nature is what we know —
Yet have no art to say —
So impotent Our Wisdom is
To her Simplicity.
— *"Nature" Is What We See*

If I can stop one heart from breaking,
I shall not live in vain;
—*If I can stop one heart from breaking*

Faith — The Experiment of Our Lord —
— *"Morning" Means "Milking" to the Farmer*

There is no frigate like a book
    To take us lands away,—
There is no frigate like a book

Gregg Tomusko

A word is dead
When it is said,
   Some say.

I say it just
Begins to live
   That day.
—*A word is dead*

As imperceptibly as grief
The summer lapsed away,
—*As imperceptibly as grief*

That those who know her, know her less
   The nearer her they get.   *(Nature)*
—*What mystery pervades a well*

He ate and drank the precious words,
His spirit grew robust;
He knew no more that he was poor,
Nor that his frame was dust.
—*He ate and drank the precious words*

The brain is wider than the sky,
—*The brain is wider than the sky*

Finite to fail, but infinite to venture.
—*Finite to fail*

I NEVER SAW A MOOR

I never saw a moor,
I never saw the sea;
Yet know I how the heather looks,
And what a wave must be.

I never spoke with God,
Nor visited in heaven;
Yet certain am I of the spot
As if the chart were given.

Emily Dickinson

Faith.

As we grow in faith, we become certain of many things we've never seen.

Incidentally, did you ever think a chart *could* be given to heaven? That it resides in a mapped location in the grand universe?

***

Lord,
Increase my faith.

I can't imagine a life without fear, to be forever confident of the Father's care. Yet that describes how you lived your life on earth, fearing no man even when being crucified by controlling and cruel men. That demonstrates great faith.

How many things we can know without seeing, as the love between a mother and child, while still here on earth. Why then, when you talk of heaven, do we question it?

I DIED FOR BEAUTY

I died for beauty, but was scarce
Adjusted in the tomb,
When one who died for truth was lain
In an adjoining room.

He questioned softly why I failed?
"For beauty," I replied.
"And I for truth, -- the two are one;
We brethren are," he said.

And so, as kinsmen met a night,
We talked between the rooms,
Until the moss had reached our lips,
And covered up our names.

Emily Dickinson

"I died for beauty" would be a fitting epitaph for Emily.

The earth may cover up these names, but not heaven.

***

Lord,

Let me live for truth, beauty, and goodness.

Let me seek these divine attributes to enhance my life and achieve something worthwhile. Let me strive for that which lasts beyond this world, as William Shakespeare and Emily Dickinson accomplished, and join them as "brethren."

THE SNAKE

A narrow fellow in the grass
Occasionally rides;
You may have met him, -- did you not,
His notice sudden is.

The grass divides as with a comb,
A spotted shaft is seen;
And then it closes at your feet
And opens further on.

He likes a boggy acre,
A floor too cool for corn.
Yet when a child, and barefoot,
I more than once, at morn,

Have passed, I thought, a whip-lash
Unbraiding in the sun, --
When, stooping to secure it,
It wrinkled, and was gone.

Several of nature's people
I know, and they know me;
I feel for them a transport
Of cordiality;

But never met this fellow,
Attended or alone,
Without a tighter breathing,
And zero at the bone.

Emily Dickinson

Yes, Emily, "zero at the bone" best describes me! Far, or near, the sight of a snake makes me freeze—a base, primordial fear I'm thankful for.

***

Lord,

We keep learning more. The infant science of ecology discovers the contribution of every creature to the balance of nature. I changed from hating snakes to realizing their importance. Help me to want to put in the effort to increase my knowledge on everything, to better understand the world and appreciate all of your creation, even snakes.

THE CHARIOT

Because I could not stop for Death,
He kindly stopped for me;
The carriage held but just ourselves
And Immortality.

We slowly drove, he knew no haste,
And I had put away
My labour, and my leisure too,
For his civility.

We passed the school where children played,
Their lessons scarcely done;
We passed the fields of gazing grain,
We passed the setting sun.

We paused before a house that seemed
A swelling on the ground;
The roof was scarcely visible,
The cornice but a mound.

Since then 'tis centuries; but each
Feels shorter than the day
I first surmised the horses' heads
Were toward eternity.

Emily Dickinson

No one looks forward to death; yet, if we knew it comes as a cordial carriage ride to a destination where time flies because we live so happily, what really do we leave behind? Our loved ones will join us in a breath.

Time needs to be measured in larger quantities as we draw closer to the Isle of Paradise.

***

Lord,

Let me not ignore death until it calls for me. Let me prepare for eternal life now, survive my body decomposing, and see a million years as a blink of an eye. I believe there will be many chariot rides as I wend through your many resting places and advancement worlds.

March   21

9:00

10:00

11:00

12:00

1:00

2:00

3:00

4:00

5:00   *Fr. Hopkins*

DINNER RESERVATION: GERARD MANLEY HOPKINS

Gerard Manley Hopkins offers his life "to the greater glory of God." He praises God for the beauty in nature. He praises God in his poems. He praises God in his prayers, in the Mass, and in his vocation as a Jesuit priest.

His words and meter spring to life, with a knack to invent words that we know the meaning of, even if the word does not exist.

Why does Gerard downplay being a great poet? Why does one with a gift pen so few verses?

The answer lies in dedicating his life to Christ. His vocation centers on being a priest: to serve Christ. His prayers and meditations emulate those of St. Ignatius, the founder of the Jesuits; to be as Christ.

Gerard's acid test answers one question: "Does this make me more like Christ?" Gerard strives to be single-minded, so views everything that does not bring him nearer to Christ as wasteful. His approach matches that of Soren Kierkegaard, the Christian and Christian philosopher.

Although Gerard praises Christ through his poetry, he regards poetry as an evasion to his more spiritual duties. Gerard also perceived the danger of pride in human accomplishments and consequent recognition. Soren sacrificed marriage. Gerard sacrificed marriage and would no longer spend time to compose awe-inspiring poetry that lasts.

I learned in the seminary that the world recognizes Gerard a great poet. I learned later that Gerard quietly served as a great priest. Gerard knows the latter counts as the more valuable credential at the gates of heaven.

His ruminations revolve around his priesthood and very little on poetry.

QUOTES OF GERARD MANLY HOPKINS

Mortal Beauty, God's Grace, Major Poems and Spiritual Writings
of Gerard Manley Hopkins

"To the greater glory of God"   (Ad Majorem Dei Gloriam)
– the motto of the Jesuits.

I do not think I have ever seen anything more beautiful than the bluebell I have been looking at. I know the beauty of our Lord by it. It[s inscape] is [mixed of] strength and grace, like an ash [tree].
pg 68, "Journal" May 12, 1870.

I have been up at Oxford just long enough to have heard fr. my father and mother in return for my letter announcing my conversion. Their answers are terrible: I cannot read them twice. If you will pray for them and me just now I shall be deeply thankful.
pg 83," Letter to Rev. Dr. John H. Newman" Oct 15, 1866.

This I say: my vocation puts before me a standard so high that a higher can be found nowhere else. The question then for me is not whether I am willing . . . to make a sacrifice of hopes of fame (let us suppose), but whether I am not to undergo a severe judgment from God . . .   for the backward glances I have given with my hand upon the plough, for the waste of time the very compositions you admire may have caused and their preoccupation of the mind which belonged to more sacred or more binding duties, for the disquiet and the thoughts of vainglory they have given rise to. A purpose may look smooth and perfect from without but be frayed and faltering from within. I have never wavered in my vocation, but I have not lived up to it. I destroyed the verse I had written when I entered the Society and meant to write no more;   . . .   But there is more peace and it is the holier lot to be unknown than to be known.
pg 101, "Letter to R.W. Dixon" October 29, 1881.

We have had for three centuries often the flower of the youth of a country in numbers enter our body: among these how many poets, how many artists of all sorts, there must have been! But there have been very few Jesuit poets . . .   For genius attracts fame and individual fame St. Ignatius looked on as the most dangerous and dazzling of all attractions . . .

pg 104, "Letter to R. W. Dixon" Dec 1, 1881.

By the by, if the English race had done nothing else, yet if they left the world the notion of a gentleman, they would have done a great service to mankind.

pg 110, "Letter to Robert Bridges" Feb. 3, 1883.

"Freedom": it is perfectly true that British freedom is the best, the only successful freedom, but that is because, with whatever drawbacks, those who have developed that freedom have done so with the aid of law and obedience to law.

pg 113, "Letter to Coventry Patmore" June 4, 1886.

If we learn no more from a Gospel or a sermon on the Gospel than to know our Lord Jesus Christ better, to be prouder of him, and to love him more we learn enough and we learn a precious lesson. He is the king to whom we are to be loyal and he is the general we are to obey. The man that says to himself as he walks: Christ is my king, Christ is my hero, I am at Christ's orders, I am his to command /, that man is a child of light –

pg 131, "Sermon For Sunday Aug. 17, 1879 11th After Pentecost, at St. Clement's."

Children as soon as they can understand ought to be told about him, that they may make him the hero of their young hearts. But there are Catholic parents that shamefully neglect their duty: the grown children of Catholics are found that scarcely know or do not know his name. Will such parents say they left instruction to the priest or the schoolmaster?   . . . It is at the father's or the mother's mouth first the little one should learn.

pg 138, "Sermon, For Sunday Evening, Nov. 23, 1879 at Bedford Leigh."

There met in Jesus Christ all things that can make man lovely and loveable.
pg 139, "Sermon, For Sunday Evening, Nov. 23, 1879 at Bedford Leigh."

God heeds all things at once. He takes more interest in a merchant's business than the merchant, in a vessel's steering than the pilot, in a lover's sweetheart than the lover, in a sick man's pain than the sufferer, in our salvation than we ourselves.
pg 158, "Sermon, For Monday Evening Oct 25, 1880."

They glorify God, but they do not know it. The birds sing to him, the thunder speaks of his terror, the lion is like his strength, the sea is like his greatness, the honey like his sweetness; they are something like him, they make him known, they tell of him, they give him glory, but they do not know they do, they do not know him, they never can, they are brute things that only think of food or think of nothing. This then is poor praise, faint reverence, slight service, dull glory. Nevertheless what they can they always do.

. . .

But man can know God, can mean to give him glory. This then was why he was made, to give God glory and to mean to give it; to praise God freely, willingly to reverence him, gladly to serve him. Man was made to give, and mean to give, God glory.
I WAS MADE FOR THIS, each one of us was made for this.
pgs 181-182, "Commentary on the Spiritual Exercises of St. Ignatius and other Spiritual Writings, Instructions, the principle or foundation."

You may say you are far from hating God; but if you live in sin you are among God's enemies, you are under Satan's standard and enlisted there; you may not like it, no wonder; you may wish to be elsewhere; but there you are, an enemy to God.
pg 183, "Commentary on the Spiritual Exercises of St. Ignatius and other Spiritual Writings, Instructions, the principle or foundation."

To lift up the hands in prayer gives God glory, but a man with a dung-fork in his hand, a woman with a sloppail, give him glory too. He is so great that all things give him glory if you mean they should. So then, my brethren, live.
pg 184, "Commentary on the Spiritual Exercises of St. Ignatius and other Spiritual Writings, Instructions, the principle or foundation."

Gregg Tomusko

Gerard Manley Hopkins Priest and Poet

I am anxious to become a Catholic.
pg 19, *Gerard Manley Hopkins Priest and Poet.*

For an interior knowledge of our Lord, Who for me was made Man, in order that I may love Him better and follow Him more closely.
 (his prayer during his Spiritual Exercises of St. Ignatius)
pg 41, *Gerard Manley Hopkins Priest and Poet.*

I am so happy, I am so happy, I am so happy.   (on his deathbed)
pg 155, *Gerard Manley Hopkins Priest and Poet.*

QUOTES FROM GERARD MANLY HOPKINS POEMS

Mortal Beauty, God's Grace

Nothing is so beautiful as spring–
—*Spring*

The world is charged with the grandeur of God.
—*God's Grandeur*

           the soil
Is bare now, nor can foot feel, being shod.
—*God's Grandeur*

And for all this, nature is never spent;
There lives the dearest freshness deep down things;
—*God's Grandeur*

       My heart in hiding
Stirred for a bird, –the achieve of, the mastery of the thing!
— *The Windhover*

As a dare-gale skylark scanted in a dull cage,
  Man's mounting spirit in his bone-house, mean house, dwells–
—*The Caged Skylark*

See, Lord, at thy service low lies here a heart
Lost, all lost in wonder at the God thou art.
—*S. Thomae Aquinatis Rhythmus Ad SS. Sacramentum*

Mark Christ our King. He knows war, served this soldiering through;
— *[The Soldier]*

  out of sight is out of mind.
—*The Lantern Out of Doors*

  foot follows kind,
—*The Lantern Out of Doors*

Glory be to God for dappled things–   (variegated, spotted)
—*Pied Beauty*

He fathers-forth whose beauty is past change:
                 Praise him.
—*Pied Beauty*

             world's wildfire, leave but ash:
—*That Nature Is a Heraclitean Fire and of the Comfort of the Resurrection*

And you were a liar, O blue March day.
—*The Loss of the Eurydice*

    Death teeming in by her portholes
Raced down decks, round messes of mortals.
—*The Loss of the Eurydice*

After-comers cannot guess the beauty been.
—*Binsey Poplars*

What would the world be, once bereft
Of wet and of wildness? Let them be left,
O let them be left, wildness and wet;
Long live the weeds and the wildness yet.
—Inversnaid

And men are meant to share
Her life as life does air.
—*The Blessed Virgin Compared to the Air We Breathe*

           cries like dead letters sent
To dearest him that lives alas! away.
— *"I Wake and Feel"*

     that year
Of now done darkness I wretch lay wrestling with (my God!) my God.
— *[Carrion Comfort]*

Why do sinners' ways prosper? and why must
Disappointment all I endeavour end?
— *[Thou Art Indeed Just, Lord]*

Wert thou my enemy, O thou my friend,
How wouldst thou worse
—[*Thou Art Indeed Just, Lord]*

Time's eunuch, and not breed one work that wakes.
Mine, O thou lord of life, send my roots rain.
—[*Thou Art Indeed Just, Lord]*

THE WINDHOVER
TO CHRIST OUR LORD

I caught this morning morning's minion, king-
    dom of daylight's dauphin, dapple-dawn-drawn Falcon, in his riding
    Of the rolling level underneath him steady air, and striding
High there, how he rung upon the rein of a wimpling wing
In his ecstasy! then off, off forth on swing,
    As a skate's heel sweeps smooth on a bow-bend: the hurl and gliding
    Rebuffed the big wind. My heart in hiding
Stirred for a bird,- the achieve of, the mastery of the thing!

Brute beauty and valour and act, oh, air, pride, plume, here
    Buckle! AND the fire that breaks from thee then, a billion
Times told lovelier, more dangerous, O my chevalier!

    No wonder of it: sheer plod makes plough down sillion
Shine, and blue-bleak embers, ah my dear,
    Fall, gall themselves, and gash gold-vermilion.

Gerard Manley Hopkins

Through an unusual meter, Father Hopkins emulates the flight of a bird. How exciting it must be to fly! How easy the bird defies gravity then hover stationary in the wind. Aspirations of beauty, valor, strength, and glory come to mind watching a falcon soar.

Christ fulfills our highest aspirations. Oh, a billion times more, though the way narrow.

Underneath it all ("plough down"), the beauty of Christ's life and ours ("sillion shine"—silica is a mineral found in quartz that makes dull rocks shine, and embers break open into "gold-vermillion," vermillion a vivid reddish orange color), manifests only by sacrifice ("fall, gall", and "gash") in our daily work of service to others.

***

Lord,

Father Hopkins truly loved you. He dedicated his life to your greater glory. He described you with such beautiful words, uplifting as watching a bird's mastery of flight, noble as working the earth to better the soil. Lord, give me the desire to labor in building your kingdom here on earth, as Father Hopkins loved to do.

GOD'S GRANDEUR

The world is charged with the grandeur of God.
　　It will flame out, like shining from shook foil;
　　It gathers to a greatness, like the ooze of oil
Crushed. Why do men then now not reck his rod?
Generations have trod, have trod, have trod;
　　And all is seared with trade; bleared, smeared with toil;
　　And wears man's smudge and shares man's smell: the soil
Is bare now, nor can foot feel, being shod.

And for all this, nature is never spent,
　　There lives the dearest freshness deep down things;
And though the last lights off the black West went
　　Oh, morning, at the brown brink eastward, springs-
Because the Holy Ghost over the bent
　　World broods with warm breast and with ah! bright wings.

Gerard Manley Hopkins

The world is *charged* with the grandeur of God. Like electricity, there exists excitement everywhere. Then why do men react so insensitively to God's grandeur, and no longer recognize His wonder of creation? With industry, we lose touch with nature and can no longer feel, our foot "being shod" in a boot.

And we are *charged* with accountability. Does the world bend down because we have crumpled it, or to bow in respect to God's law? We still have hope, because nature retains "the dearest freshness deep down" and the Holy Ghost "broods" over us, much as a mother hen would do for her chicks.

***

Lord,

I've learned to love nature. In lush valleys water cascades off a mountain top, flowing with a wonder and freshness that stirs the spirit in my breast, leading to contemplation of your grandeur. No wonder you loved beautiful places, and chose them for your intimate meetings with our Father.

BINSEY POPLARS
FELLED 1879

My aspens dear, whose airy cages quelled,
Quelled or quenched in leaves the leaping sun,
All felled, felled, are all felled;
   Of a fresh and following folded rank
         Not spared, not one
         That dandled a sandalled
      Shadow that swam or sank
On meadow and river and wind-wandering weed-winding bank.

O if we but knew what we do
      When we delve or hew-
   Hack and rack the growing green!
      Since country is so tender
To touch, her being so slender,
That, like this sleek and seeing ball
But a prick will make no eye at all,
Where we, even where we mean
        To mend her we end her,
   When we hew or delve:
After-comers cannot guess the beauty been.
   Ten or twelve, only ten or twelve
   Strokes of havoc unselve
     The sweet especial scene,
   Rural scene, a rural scene,
   Sweet especial rural scene.

Gerard Manley Hopkins

We recently discovered ecology and, while still in an infant state, how much it already contributes to our appreciation of the complex balance in nature. We revived Homeopathic medicine and realize the final cure for cancer we may have just hacked down. We hardly know what we are doing.

The human eye we appreciate as a miraculous creation. We work very careful around our eyes, and best leave them alone, lest we lose the precious gift of vision. What better analogy to the especial and sweet nature we find in rural settings.

I once walked my dogs in the beautiful woods behind my home. Today, there are huge houses. Did my home appreciate? I would no longer buy it and "After-comers cannot guess the beauty been."

***

Lord,

If I could build a house that looks over a pastoral scene, why wouldn't I?

Help me to be that rare individual that purchases the land and gives it to the parks for the preservation of nature. Millionaires have done this for mankind. I would guess they are well established in your kingdom of eternal beauty.

(THOU ART INDEED JUST, LORD)

Justus quidem tu es, Domine, si disputem tecum: verumtamen
justa loquar ad te: Quare via impiorum prosperatur? etc.
(Righteous art thou, O Lord, when I plead with thee: yet let me talk with thee
of thy judgments: Wherefore doth the way of the wicked prosper?   – Jeremiah
xii.1)

Thou art indeed just, Lord, if I contend
With thee; but, sir, so what I plead is just.
Why do sinners' ways prosper? and why must
Disappointment all I endeavour end?
      Wert thou my enemy, O thou my friend,
How wouldst thou worse, I wonder, than thou dost
Defeat, thwart me? Oh, the sots and thralls of lust
Do in spare hours more thrive than I that spend,
Sir, life upon thy cause, See, banks and brakes
Now, leaved how thick! laced they are again
With fretty chervil, look, and fresh wind shakes
Them; birds build – but not I build; no, but strain,
Time's eunuch, and not breed one work that wakes.
Mine, O thou lord of life, send my roots rain.

Gerard Manley Hopkins

A perplexing question persists: "Why does good fail?" This poem provides an answer to the apparent failure of goodness—the verse, filled with the attributes of God survives whereas the sins of people from Father Hopkins's time we forget.

On our confused world, we find it difficult to believe that working for the good can be effective. In God's well-organized universe it becomes obvious good does triumph.

***

Lord,

Evil scores victories every day. The good get pushed aside and ignored. We're down here—where you were hassled, suffered injustices, and brutally murdered. How does good win?

I know good does triumph in your kingdom, but your kingdom exists not on earth. I guess that's why we pray "thy kingdom come, thy will be done, on earth as it is in heaven." Surely your kingdom will reign here someday.

March   23

9:00   *Spiritual Renewal — Church Hall*

10:00   *All day Saturday and Sunday*

11:00

12:00

1:00

2:00

3:00

4:00

5:00

Gregg Tomusko

LORD, TEACH US TO PRAY

Lord, teach us to pray
It's been a long and cold December-kind of day
With our hearts and hands all busy, in our private little wars,
We stand and watch each other now, from separate shores –
We lose the way.

I need to know today the way things should be in my head.
I need to know for once now, the things that should be said.
I've got to learn to walk around as if I were not dead.
I've got to find a way to learn to live.

Lord, teach us to pray
It's been a long and cold December-kind of day
With our hearts and hands all busy, in our private little wars,
We stand and watch each other now, from separate shores –
We lose the way.

I still get so distracted, by the color of my skin.
I still get so upset now, when I find that I don't win.
I meet so many strangers, I'm so slow to take them in.
I've got to find a way to really live.

Lord, teach us to pray
It's been a long and cold December-kind of day
With our hearts and hands all busy, in our private little wars,
We stand and watch each other now, from separate shores –
We lose the way.

I stand so safe and sterile, as I watch a man fall flat.
I'm silent with a man who'd like to know just where I'm at.
With the aged and the lonely, I can barely tip my hat.
I need to see the sin of "I don't care".

Kristofferson and Yeats

Lord, teach us to pray
It's been a long and cold December-kind of day
With our hearts and hands all busy, in our private little wars,
We stand and watch each other now, from separate shores –
We lose the way.

I stand so smug and sure before the people I've outguessed.
To let a man be who he is, I still see as a test.
And when it all comes down to must, I'm sure my way is best.
I've got to find what 'room' means in my heart.

Lord, teach us to pray
It's been a long and cold December-kind of day
With our hearts and hands all busy, in our private little wars,
We stand and watch each other now, from separate shores –
We lose the way.

I walk and fall myself alone, can't tolerate a guide.
And when the camps split up, I'm sure to put you on my side.
And dare someone to challenge me, and swear I will not hide.
I've got to find a better way to live.

Lord, teach us to pray
It's been a long and cold December-kind of day
With our hearts and hands all busy, in our private little wars,
We stand and watch each other now, from separate shores –
We lose the way.

I'm out so many things, take so little time to weigh.
I've let it all slip by, in the sweep of yesterday.
I can't believe you mean it all, to grace me on my way.
I've got to find a way to really live.

Lord, teach us to pray
We still believe that we can find a better way.
Teach us to pray.
We lose the way.
Teach us to pray.

Joe Wise

The apostles asked Jesus to teach them to pray.

We lack the brains to even consider that we need to pray. Hence the recurring request, "Lord, teach us to pray," to create a desire in us to even want to pray. We believe that we can find a better way alone. Our salvation lies not in total self-reliance, but in complete dependence on God.

I feel self-satisfied until I hear these lyrics. This presents a different evaluation than my usual examination, and I fall short. Yet this probably comes closer to what God expects of us.

***

Lord,

How many of us does this song describe? Any verse fits me perfectly. But why alter my thinking, all my hard-to-come-by survival skills, only to start losing things in this world? I would have to be attracted to something far better before considering changing.

I guess that's what prayer does: to allow one to see something, and someone, vastly superior.

ONE DAY AT A TIME

I'm only human, I'm just a man.
Help me believe in what I could be and all that I am.
Show me the stairway I have to climb.
Lord, for my sake, teach me to take
One day at a time.

One day at a time, sweet Jesus, that's all I'm asking from you.
Just give me the strength to do ev'ry day what I have to do.
Yesterday's gone, sweet Jesus, and tomorrow may never be mine.
Lord, help me today, show me the way
One day at a time.

Do you remember when you walked among men
Well, Jesus, you know if you're looking below that it's worse now than then
Pushin' and shovin', crowding my mind
So for my sake, Lord, teach me to take
One day at a time.

Marijohn Wilkin and Kris Kristofferson

"Sufficient unto the day is the evil thereof." Our creator advised us to take one day at a time. He promised us to go through each day, all of life's ups and downs, together.

***

Lord,

I just watched an interview with Tom Jones, and he disclosed that Elvis would come to his Vegas act and join him on stage, and after the show they would sing Gospel songs all night long. One of their favorites was "One Day at a Time."

Elvis loved you, Jesus. For people who are great at something, to acknowledge all they have comes due to you, inspires, and puts us back on track.

Teach me to live loyally today, and then will tomorrow take care of itself.

Gregg Tomusko

LORD, WHEN YOU CAME

Lord, when you came to the seashore
You weren't seeking the wise or the wealthy,
But only asking that I might follow.

O Lord, in my eyes you were gazing,
Kindly smiling, my name you were saying;
All I treasured, I have left on the sand there;
Close to you, I will find other seas.

Lord, you knew what my boat carried:
Neither money nor weapons for fighting,
But nets for fishing, my daily labor.

O Lord, in my eyes you were gazing,
Kindly smiling, my name you were saying;
All I treasured, I have left on the sand there;
Close to you, I will find other seas.

Lord, have you need of my labor,
Hands for service, a heart made for loving,
My arms for lifting the poor and broken?

O Lord, in my eyes you were gazing,
Kindly smiling, my name you were saying;
All I treasured, I have left on the sand there;
Close to you, I will find other seas.

Lord, send me where you would have me,
To a village, or heart of the city;
I will remember that you are with me.

O Lord, in my eyes you were gazing,
Kindly smiling, my name you were saying;
All I treasured, I have left on the sand there;
Close to you, I will find other seas.

Cesareo Gabarain

The Lord calling individuals has not changed since he walked on the seashore and spoke to some fishermen, "Come, and follow me." It's not much to go on!

The Spirit convinces us to answer his call. And only a deepening love for Jesus keeps us from turning back and carping, "Forget this!"

Our hearts burn and our eyes well up as Jesus gazes into our eyes and says our name. To feel loved that deeply we change, willing to leave all we treasured to follow him.

***

Lord,

After all these years, I still have pitiful little to offer you. I see you gazing into my eyes with so much love. I want to always ask why, why would you love me?

Help me to leave things and follow you. I'm still scared to, and perhaps only death will finally force me to part with everything.

Gregg Tomusko

AMAZING GRACE

Amazing grace! how sweet the sound
   That saved a wretch like me!
I once was lost, but now am found,
   Was blind, but now I see.

'Twas grace that taught my heart to fear,
   And grace my fears relieved;
How precious did that grace appear
   The hour I first believed.

Through many dangers, toils, and snares
   I have already come;
'Tis grace hath brought me safe thus far,
   And grace will lead me home.

The Lord has promised good to me,
   His word my hope secures;
He will my shield and portion be
   As long as life endures.

When we've been there ten thousand years
   Bright shining as the sun
We've no less days to sing God's praise
   Than when we'd first begun.

John Newton   John P. Rees (last verse)

What better adjective for grace than "amazing?" There have been thousands of witnesses whose ruined lives were totally transformed in an instant by grace, who describe the change as amazing. To all, the healing that results from divine forgiveness, as the son returns to the Father, points to the efficacious fruit of grace. By this grace we begin our long journey toward our Father in heaven. And this grace will sustain us.

Since we are given the gift of eternal life, our long journey here we will someday view as "being over with so quickly," all because of grace.

***

Lord,

Many believers list this as their favorite song because they know how precious grace has been to their lives.

I know grace as a gift from God, that which changes lives and what brings heaven on earth.

Lord, through your grace, let me figure out how I can build up your kingdom and then have the courage to do so. Let my soul be filled with your grace so that I please you.

Gregg Tomusko

WERE YOU THERE

Were you there when they crucified my Lord?
Were you there when they crucified my Lord?
Oh! Sometimes it causes me to tremble, tremble, tremble!
Were you there when they crucified my Lord?

Were you there when they nailed him to the tree?
Were you there when they nailed him to the tree?
Oh! Sometimes it causes me to tremble, tremble, tremble!
Were you there when they nailed him to the tree?

Were you there when they pierced him in the side?
Were you there when they pierced him in the side?
Oh! Sometimes it causes me to tremble, tremble, tremble!
Were you there when they pierced him in the side?

Were you there when the sun refused to shine?
Were you there when the sun refused to shine?
Oh! Sometimes it causes me to tremble, tremble, tremble!
Were you there when the sun refused to shine?

Were you there when they laid him in the tomb?
Were you there when they laid him in the tomb?
Oh! Sometimes it causes me to tremble, tremble, tremble!
Were you there when they laid him in the tomb?

Were you there when he rose from out the tomb?
Were you there when he rose from out the tomb?
Oh! Sometimes it causes me to tremble, tremble, tremble!
Were you there when he rose from out the tomb?

Negro Spiritual

This song puts me in front of the cross, which causes me to tremble.

Since I'm there, I decide to tag along with the young apostle John, so I can say "I was there." I did not really expect Jesus to rise from the dead, though he spoke of it and I believe what he says. After witnessing the humiliation and cruel suffering, his death looked so final.

I trembled and trembled in awe and hope-fulfilled excitement when I actually viewed our risen Lord.

***

Lord,

Goode (Old English for holy) Friday, we distinguish as the saddest day on earth. We creatures killed our loving creator. How screwed up can we be? What kind of animal did we become? But that misses the lesson. Like your glorious resurrection, Jesus, you tell us we are sons and daughters of God. We need only faith to transform into what we are.

April   **5**

9:00   *(Day of meditation and reflection)*

10:00

11:00

12:00

1:00

2:00

3:00

4:00

5:00

I REMEMBER, I REMEMBER

I remember, I remember,
The house where I was born,
The little window where the sun
Came peeping in at morn;
He never came a wink too soon,
Nor brought too long a day,
But now, I often wish the night
Had borne my breath away!

I remember, I remember,
The roses, red and white,
The vi'lets, and the lily-cups,
Those flowers made of light!
The lilacs where the robin built,
And where my brother set
The laburnum on his birthday, –
The tree is living yet!

I remember, I remember,
Where I was used to swing,
And thought the air must rush as fresh
To swallows on the wing;
My spirit flew in feathers then,
That is so heavy now,
And summer pools could hardly cool
The fever on my brow!

I remember, I remember,
The fir trees dark and high;
I used to think their slender tops
Were close against the sky:
It was a childish ignorance,
But now 'tis little joy
To know I'm farther off from heav'n
Than when I was a boy.

Thomas Hood

I set aside Good Friday as a day of personal reflection. What would I have done if I saw the Lord pass by? If I witnessed the crucifixion, what would have been my thoughts? If I were there, would I prefer to be a child or an adult standing by the cross? Did I lose something essential while growing up?

I remember that as a child I felt clothed in love. On my first communion I enjoyed a peaceful, intimate closeness to Jesus. The world looked happy and dressed in bright colors. As a young adult, I tried to regain that personal contact with Jesus that once made me so happy. In the seminary, I again felt peace and a great love, but the world outside, with a war raging in Vietnam, hovered never far from my thoughts. As an adult, the tables turn and it is God who, though never too far from my thoughts remains "outside" from what I am doing and no longer first on my to-do list.

It counts as little consolation that I felt closer to God as a boy than as a man.

***

Lord,

We're meant to grow closer to you as we grow up; not further away. But as you explained, we need to be born again, begin anew in the life of the spirit, and maintain a child-like trust and wonder, even as we assume more earthly responsibilities; and not merely grow older.

WHAT WOULD I GIVE?

What would I give for a heart of flesh to warm me through,
Instead of this heart of stone ice-cold whatever I do;
Hard and cold and small, of all hearts the worst of all.

What would I give for words, if only words would come;
But now in its misery my spirit has fallen dumb:
Oh, merry friends, go your way, I have never a word to say.

What would I give for tears, not smiles but scalding tears,
To wash the black mark clean, and to thaw the frost of years,
To wash the stain ingrain and to make me clean again.

Christina Rossetti

Ah, the depths of sorrow and its effect on the human personality.

If, as a one-time offer, I could choose a prize of $10 million or the forgiveness of a sin that causes me great sorrow, which would I choose?

Intellectually and experientially, I understand how important it means to be happy, to know gratitude in my heart, to possess friends that I can speak openly with, to live through moments of peace in troubled times, to love and be loved, and to maintain a conscience free from offense. I value spiritual gifts; yet, I would still feel a fool to turn down ten million.

***

Lord,
   Let my confessions be as contrite. Let my soul be exposed so I can see it as clear as you do.

Lord, make my soul a clean abode; a room where you'd want to stay.

April 7

Easter Sunday

9:00 *Easter Sunday Mass*

10:00

11:00

12:00

1:00 *Easter Dinner*

2:00

3:00

4:00

5:00

SPRING

Nothing is so beautiful as spring –
    When weeds, in wheels, shoot long and lovely and lush;
    Thrush's eggs look little low heavens, and thrush
Through the echoing timber does so rinse and wring
The ear, it strikes like lightnings to hear him sing;
    The glassy peartree leaves and blooms, they brush
    The descending blue; that blue is all in a rush
With richness; the racing lambs too have fair their fling.

What is all this juice and all this joy?
    A strain of the earth's sweet being in the beginning
In Eden garden. – Have, get, before it cloy,
    Before it cloud, Christ, lord, and sour with sinning,
Innocent mind and Mayday in girl and boy,
Most, O maid's child, thy choice and worthy the winning.

Gerard Manley Hopkins

After so long a winter, nothing arrives so beautiful as spring. What we thought dead arises into new, exciting, and colorful life. If we desire this new life, as once flourished in the Garden of Eden, we need to seek Mary's son, who is the life and the way.

***

Lord,

I love the seasons. After a bleak and cold winter, who would think of a spring, full of green and vibrant life? After suffering and death, who would think of a resurrection, of life after physical death? One we call glorious.

Let us learn from nature, to live simple and innocent as in the first garden, so the full impact of spring's rebirth may infuse new life into our every cell. Let us experience the spiritual fullness of Easter and Pentecost.

EASTER SYMBOL

Oh, lily, symbol of the risen One . . .
Harbinger of the cleansing spring
Of each new year . . .
Sweet-scented flower,
Your purity doth chasten, smite
The careless ones.
Serenity on stately stem,
You halt our step . . .
Reminding us of prayer.

Ella Castle Nedrow

A pure white lily, that resurrects itself each Easter, cannot help but remind us of Christ.

Certainly, someone divine had a hand in creation. The flowers cry out, in symphony and song to the risen Jesus, who appears in the beauty of the lilies, in the midst of the trumpeters!

***

Lord,

Was the lily created to remind us of you? A lily resurrects itself in a glorious form every spring, dazzling white like your transfiguration, and pure and lovely as you.

KEEP IN MIND

Keep in mind that Jesus Christ has died for us and is risen from the dead.
He is our saving Lord, he is joy for all ages.

Rev. Lucien Deiss, CSSp

In few words, the entire Christian faith is summarized. What better way to keep faith alive than to keep these words in mind. We appropriately sing this at Communion, for at the Last Supper Jesus asked us that when we break bread together to remember his life that he lived here among us.

***

Lord,

Let me keep you in mind, so close that I feel your presence throughout the day, hear your words of comfort, and enjoy that peace and happiness we call joy.

May

12

Mother's Day

9:00

10:00

11:00

12:00

1:00   *Dinner at Mom's*

2:00

3:00

4:00

5:00

PARENTS PRAYER

They are little only once Lord. Grant me the wisdom
    and patience to teach them to follow in your footsteps
    and prepare them for what is to come.

They are little only once Lord. Make me take the time
    to play pretend, to read or tell a story; to cuddle.
    Don't let me for one minute think anything is more
    important than the school play, the recital, the big
    game, fishing or the quiet walk hand in hand.
    All too soon Lord they will grow away and there is no
    turning back. Let me have my memories with no regrets.

Please help me be a good parent, Lord. When I must
    discipline -- let me do it in love, let me be firm, but fair;
    let me correct and explain with patience.

They are growing away Lord. While I have the chance
    let me do my best for them. For the rest of our lives,
    please lord, let me be their very best friend.

Mary Loveridge Robbins

I watched my daughter socialize in preschool, and grew bored, concerned that I was wasting my time. I read this poem placed on the wall, which reminded me how quickly my son had grown up. I became more actively involved in my daughter's play.

The only thing I can remember doing this past month is playing with my daughter in preschool. And I am thankful that in the past I did the same with my son.

My wife seems to naturally possess the perspective of this poem, and immerses herself in whatever the children consider important.

***

Lord,

I pray mothers take the time to raise their children; to sacrifice all—career, personal interests, social lives—for the good of their children, as you did when you came to earth and spent all of your time raising your spiritual children on earth.

May

30

Memorial Day

9:00

10:00   *Memorial Day Parade*

11:00   *(after—speeches, coffee and donuts—behind City Hall)*

12:00

1:00

2:00

3:00

4:00

5:00

A NAMELESS GRAVE

"A soldier of the Union mustered out,"
Is the inscription on an unknown grave
At Newport News, beside the salt-sea wave,
Nameless and dateless; sentinel or scout
Shot down in skirmish, or disastrous rout
Of battle, when the loud artillery drave
Its iron wedges through the ranks of brave
And doomed battalions, storming the redoubt.
Thou unknown hero sleeping by the sea
In thy forgotten grave! with secret shame
I feel my pulses beat, my forehead burn,
When I remember thou hast given for me
All that thou hadst, thy life, thy very name,
And I can give thee nothing in return.

Henry Wadsworth Longfellow

Every speech on this day of memorial should contain one key sentiment: "Thou hast given for me all that thou hadst . . . . And I can give thee nothing in return."

***

Jesus,

No greater love hath any man that he lay down his life for his fellows. Thank you for showing us this great love. Bless the soldier who follows your footsteps.

A Christian woman who lost her home and freedom and whose life remains endangered by radical Islam writes a fitting tribute to our soldiers:
A Note of thanks
This book would not be complete without a special thank you to our military.

Words tremble on my lips and emotions swell in my heart in my attempt to humbly thank you for all the things you do to protect America and the world. Words cannot express my depth of gratitude to your service, to your sacrifice, to all that you leave behind to go forth into the world and protect America's interests around the globe.

Let my grateful tears thank you for the nights you slept freezing in a tent or sweating in the desert, for the lonely days you spent missing your loved ones, for the hours you spent sick in pain and without someone holding your hand, for the moments of sheer fright in the heart of battle, for the wounds you have suffered fighting evil, for the endless days in hospitals undergoing painful surgeries, for the precious occasions you have missed back at home. For all of these sacrifices I thank you on behalf of millions of Americans who are so grateful for you. We truly appreciate these sacrifices.

A special thank you is in order to your families, to the parents who raised you and made you the man or woman you are today. I thank your wives, husbands, and your loved ones who stand by you and support you with their love and dedication.

And for those who returned in eternal sleep, may your legacy be honored for generations to come, may the tears shed over your coffins fertilize the fields of patriotism in our nation to raise a new generation built on strength and honor, able and willing to follow in your footsteps when duty calls to defend America. May your blood not have been shed in vain. May we prove worthy of your sacrifice. May we always honor your parents so they will always know that they are the parents of an American hero.

You are our brave ones, our heroes, and our national treasures. You are the pride of our nation, our strength, and our foundation. Thanks to you, millions have been freed around the world, Thanks to you, those who criticize our country, burn our precious flag, and speak ill of you, are able to do so because their freedom is built upon your blood and your sacrifice.

I salute you one and all. I bow before you in respect and humility. May God bless you and bless America, land of the free and home of the brave, and the dream that became my address.

Brigitte Gabriel
Excerpt from *They Must Be Stopped*
Why We Must Defeat Radical Islam. How We Can Do It.

June

16

Father's Day

9:00

10:00

11:00

12:00

1:00

2:00

3:00   *Favorite Poems for fathers — John's house*

4:00

5:00

THE CHILDREN'S HOUR

Between the dark and the daylight,
    When the night is beginning to lower,
Comes a pause in the day's occupations,
    That is known as the Children's Hour.

I hear in the chamber above me
    The patter of little feet,
The sound of a door that is opened,
    And voices soft and sweet.

From my study I see in the lamplight,
    Descending the broad hall stair,
Grave Alice, and laughing Allegra,
    And Edith with golden hair.

A whisper, and then a silence:
    Yet I know by their merry eyes
They are plotting and planning together
    To take me by surprise.

A sudden rush from the stairway,
    A sudden raid from the hall!
By three doors left unguarded
    They enter my castle wall!

They climb up into my turret
    O'er the arms and back of my chair;
If I try to escape, they surround me;
    They seem to be everywhere.

They almost devour me with kisses,
    Their arms about me entwine,
Till I think of the Bishop of Bingen
    In his Mouse-Tower on the Rhine!

Do you think, O blue-eyed banditti,
    Because you have scaled the wall,
Such an old mustache as I am
    Is not a match for you all!

I have you fast in my fortress,
    And will not let you depart,
But put you down into the dungeon
    In the round-tower of my heart.

And there will I keep you forever,
    Yes, forever and a day,
Till the walls shall crumble to ruin,
    And moulder in dust away!

Henry Wadsworth Longfellow

A well-planned attack in the study, full of stealth and glee, plays out as but a trap, as a father's heart and imagination again gets captured by "capturing" his children. What fun this poem is! What a celebration of the ways of children.

***

Father,

Let me love and pray for my children my entire life. And when it is over, let all of us children live with you, our one, true, and good heavenly Father.

PIANO

Softly, in the dusk, a woman is singing to me;
Taking me back down the vista of years, till I see
A child sitting under the piano, in the boom of the tingling strings
And pressing the small, poised feet of a mother who smiles as she sings.

In spite of myself, the insidious mastery of song
Betrays me back, till the heart of me weeps to belong
To the old Sunday evenings at home, with winter outside
And hymns in the cosy parlour, the tinkling piano our guide.

So now it is vain for the singer to burst into clamour
With the great black piano appassionato. The glamour
Of childish days is upon me, my manhood is cast
Down in the flood of remembrance, I weep like a child for the past.

D.H. Lawrence

"You walk in here a full-grown man, and leave a little child."

Some reminders of childhood, like exploring newfound woods and follow a remote rivulet, lighting a candle in a late night mass, or hearing a song we heard when seven, transforms us back to a blessed day when our mothers so loved and protected us.

***

Lord,

Thank you for the love of a mother. We will never experience a love like that again until we find ourselves as little children living in your eternal home.

SONNET 73

That time of year thou mayst in me behold
When yellow leaves, or none, or few, do hang
Upon those boughs which shake against the cold,
Bare ruined choirs, where late the sweet birds sang.
In me thou see'st the twilight of such day
As after sunset fadeth in the west;
Which by and by black night doth take away,
Death's second self, that seals up all in rest.
In me thou see'st the glowing of such fire,
That on the ashes of his youth doth lie,
As the deathbed whereon it must expire,
Consumed with that which it was nourished by.
This thou perceiv'st, which makes thy love more strong,
To love that well which thou must leave ere long.

William Shakespeare

The four unique seasons compare favorably with the "seasons" of a loving relationship, and the human condition itself—the excitement of spring, golden days of summer, more mellow autumn, and finally the "end of life" in winter; everything looks cold and dark, but within each snow-covered home resides a family in front of a warm and glowing fire, fondly reminiscing cherished moments gone by, and anticipating another wonderful day.

***

Lord,

Let me love this life and all the loving relationships that I'll be leaving behind, and then cheerfully move on to where my relationship with you grows deeper, full knowing all my past relationships survive death.

Kristofferson and Yeats

ON HIS SEVENTY-FIFTH BIRTHDAY

I strove with none; for none was worth my strife.
Nature I loved, and next to Nature, Art;
I warmed both hands before the fire of life;
It sinks, and I am ready to depart.

Walter Savage Landor

Truth can sound a bit cold. When one has little time left, it's best to state just what you mean. Here we have a man content with his approach to life, and recognizes that his life will be extinguished soon.

***

Lord,

Let me see this life as sitting beside a fire and warming my hands, and when the fire dies, to gladly depart into the warmth of the Holy Spirit, whose fire now enkindles forever in my heart.

June 20

9:00

10:00

11:00

12:00

1:00

2:00 *Town Hall—Open Forum!*

3:00

4:00

5:00

DESPERADOS WAITING FOR THE TRAIN

I'd play "The Red River Valley"
And he'd sit out in the kitchen and cry,
And run his fingers through seventy years of livin'
And wonder, "Lord, has ev'ry well I drilled run dry?"
We were friends, me and this old man;
Like desperados waiting for the train,
Like desperados waiting for the train.

He's a drifter and a driller of oil wells,
And an old-school man of the world.
He let me drive his car when he's too drunk to,
And he'd wink and give me money for the girls.
And our lives were like some old western movie;
Like desperados waiting for the train,
Like desperados waiting for the train.

From the time that I could walk, he'd take me with him
To a bar called The Green Frog Cafe,
And there were old men with beer guts and dominos
Lyin' about their lives while they'd play.
And I was just a kid they called his sidekick.
Like desperados waiting for the train,
Like desperados waiting for the train.

One day I looked up and he's pushin' eighty
And there's brown tobacco stains all down his chin.
To me, he's one of the heroes of this country;
So why's he all dressed up like them old men,
Drinkin' beer and playin' "Moon and Forty-Two?"
Like desperados waiting for the train,
Like desperados waiting for the train.

The day before he died, I went to see him.
I was grown, and he was almost gone.
So we just closed our eyes and dreamed us up a kitchen,
And sang another verse to that old song.
Come on, Jack, that son of a gun's a-comin'.
Like desperados waiting for the train,
Like desperados waiting for the train.

Guy Clark

We call some heroes because of their hearts, some their minds, some their courage, some their service, and some their backbones. This life does provide a lot of experiences, good and bad. It also leaves heroes to care for themselves even though they embody a living history.

***

Heavenly Father,

Friendship plays an important part in our lives. Let me take the time to care about others and form friendships where we cheer each other along the way.

Kristofferson and Yeats

OLD DOGS, CHILDREN AND WATERMELON WINE

"How old do you think I am?" he said
I said "well, I didn't know."
He said "I turned 65
About eleven months ago."

I was sittin' in Miami,
Pourin' blended whiskey down
When this old, grey black gentleman
Was cleanin' up the lounge.

There wasn't anyone around
'cept this old man and me.
The guy who ran the bar
Was watchin' 'Ironsides' on T.V.

Uninvited, he sat down
And opened up his mind
On old dogs and children,
And watermelon wine.

"Ever had a drink
Of watermelon wine?", he asked.
He told me all about it
Though I didn't answer back.

Ain't but three things in this world
That's worth a solitary dime,
But old dogs - children,
And watermelon wine.

He said "women think about theyselves
When men folk ain't around,
And friends are hard to find
When they discover that you down."

He said "I tried it all,
When I was young and in my natural prime;
Now it's old dogs – children
And watermelon wine.

Old dogs care about you
Even when you make mistakes,
God bless little children
While there still too young to hate."

When he moved away,
I found my pen and copied down that line
'bout old dogs and children
And watermelon wine.

I had to catch a plane
Up to Atlanta that next day,
As I left for my room
I saw him pickin' up my change.

That night I dreamed in peaceful sleep
Of shady summertime
Of old dogs and children
And watermelon wine.

Tom T. Hall

As we grow older, we know a little more about ourselves, our likes and dislikes. A lot of illusions dispel and we are left with only a handful of things we truly love. I find it interesting to listen to old people and discover what they still treasure after all those years.

I believe this happened, just as related in this song. And I like this man's choices.

***

God,

Dogs provide so much fun. They're always happy to see us and excited about everything.

Children arrive trusting, bright eyed, and innocent. You call them precious.

I've always wanted to try watermelon wine, but it sells out so fast. Must be good!

Lord, thank you for these three wonderful blessings.

Gregg Tomusko

TO RAMONA

Ramona, come closer,
Shut softly your watery eyes.
The pangs of your sadness
Shall pass as your senses will rise.
The flowers of the city,
Though breath-like, get death-like at times.
And there's no use in tryin'
T' deal with the dyin',
Though I cannot explain that in lines.

Your cracked country lips
I still wish to kiss
As to be under the strength of your skin
Your magnetic movements
Still capture the minutes I'm in
But it grieves my heart, love
To see you tryin' to be a part of
A world that just don't exist
It's all just a dream, babe
A vacuum, a scheme, babe
That sucks you into feelin' like this

I can see that your head
Has been twisted and fed
By worthless foam from the mouth
I can tell you are torn
Between stayin' and returnin'
On back to the South.
You've been fooled into thinking
That the finishin' end is at hand
Yet there's no one to beat you
No one t' defeat you
'Cept the thoughts of yourself feeling bad

I've heard you say many times
That you're better'n no one
And no one is better'n you
If you really believe that
You know you got
Nothing to win and nothing to lose

From fixtures and forces and friends
Your sorrow does stem
That hype you and type you
Making you feel
That you must be exactly like them

I'd forever talk to you
But soon my words
They would turn into a meaningless ring
For deep in my heart
I know there is no help I can bring
Everything passes
Everything changes
Just do what you think you should do
And someday maybe
Who knows, baby
I'll come and be cryin' to you

Bob Dylan

Some live in a dream world, often becoming inveterate liars, or look to attach themselves to a chosen liberal cause, or become emotionally involved in a popular feeling. A few laconic, raw adjectives may snap a person out of this state. However, some prosper in their unreal world, remain happy, and surpass those who assume the burden of reality.

***

Lord,

Some seem on the fringes of reality, losing themselves in a crowd, merging in with popular movements, or living only within the boundaries of their own little world. Their politics cause frustration to those who face harsh reality.

Lord, help us to experience life without illusions or excuses, to face it head on as you did. We exist here to experience things, and if we end up victorious over glamour and lies, we will be better prepared to serve in your eternal kingdom.

Gregg Tomusko

MY BACK PAGES

Crimson flames tied through my ears
Rollin' high and mighty traps
Pounced with fire on flaming roads
Using ideas as my maps
"We'll meet on edges, soon," said I
Proud 'neath heated brow.
Ah, but I was so much older then,
I'm younger than that now.

Half-wracked prejudice leaped forth
"Rip down all hate," I screamed
Lies that life is black and white
Spoke from my skull. I dreamed
Romantic facts of musketeers
Foundationed deep, somehow
Ah, but I was so much older then
I'm younger than that now

Girls' faces formed the forward path
From phony jealousy
To memorizing politics
Of ancient history
Flung down by corpse evangelists
Unthought of, though, somehow
Ah, but I was so much older then
I'm younger than that now

A self-ordained professor's tongue
Too serious to fool
Spouted out that liberty
Is just equality in school
"Equality," I spoke the word
As if a wedding vow
Ah, but I was so much older then
I'm younger than that now

Kristofferson and Yeats

In a soldier's stance, I aimed my hand
At the mongrel dogs who teach
Fearing not that I'd become my enemy
In the instant that I preach
My pathway led by confusion boats
Mutiny from stern to bow
Ah, but I was so much older then
I'm younger than that now.

Yes, my guard stood hard when abstract threats
Too noble to neglect
Deceived me into thinking
I had something to protect
Good and bad, I define these terms
Quite clear, no doubt, somehow
Ah, but I was so much older then
I'm younger than that now

Bob Dylan

Although many mapped Bob Dylan as a leader of the turbulent and revolutionary 60s, this "other side" reveals someone taking on a very critical stance of those times. Too much degeneracy tore down that separating wall of high-sounding rhetoric.

"Ah, but I was so much older then, I'm younger than that now."

When I graduated from college, I knew so much. Some of my parent's views were an embarrassment. I felt so old and so wise. Then I taught in the inner city. My parents *were* experienced and wise. I was not.

I went for my master's degree, and learned more the first quarter than the prior four years. I knew one hundred times more things then, and fully realized that one hundred times an epsilon still results in a very small amount.

I'm not sure I'm even making progress now. I encounter so little I'm able to solve. But I do stand poised ever willing to pray.

***

Heavenly Father,

As highly intelligent scholars, filled with high-brow philosophies, we could be convinced of anything. How can we protect our minds from believing things that cannot be true? How can sound youths become followers of Hitler or Bin Laden? Can we be taken in so easily into evil's grasp? Give us the courage to face the bullet, rather than to obey such leaders.

SNAKE

A snake came to my water-trough
On a hot, hot day, and I in pyjamas for the heat,
To drink there.

In the deep, strange-scented shade of the great dark carob tree
I came down the steps with my pitcher
And must wait, must stand and wait, for there he was at the trough before me.

He reached down from a fissure in the earth-wall in the gloom
And trailed his yellow-brown slackness soft-bellied down, over the edge of the stone trough
And rested his throat upon the stone bottom,
And where the water had dripped from the tap, in a small clearness,
He sipped with his straight mouth,
Softly drank through his straight gums, into his slack long body,
Silently.

Someone was before me at my water-trough,
And I, like a second-comer, waiting.

He lifted his head from his drinking, as cattle do,
And looked at me vaguely, as drinking cattle do,
And flickered his two-forked tongue from his lips, and mused a moment,
And stooped and drank a little more,
Being earth-brown, earth-golden from the burning bowels of the earth
On the day of Sicilian July, with Etna smoking.

The voice of my education said to me
He must be killed,
For in Sicily the black, black snakes are innocent, the gold are venomous.

And voices in me said, If you were a man
You would take a stick and break him now, and finish him off.

But must I confess how I liked him,
How glad I was he had come like a guest in quiet, to drink at my water-trough
And depart peaceful, pacified, and thankless
Into the burning bowels of this earth?

Was it cowardice, that I dared not kill him?
Was it perversity, that I longed to talk to him?
Was it humility, to feel so honoured?
I felt so honoured.

And yet those voices:
If you were not afraid, you would kill him!

And truly I was afraid, I was most afraid,
But even so, honoured still more
That he should seek my hospitality
From out the dark door of the secret earth.

He drank enough
And lifted his head, dreamily, as one who has drunken,
And flickered his tongue like a forked night on the air, so black,
Seeming to lick his lips,
And looked around like a god, unseeing, into the air,
And slowly turned his head,
And slowly, very slowly, as if thrice adream
Proceeded to draw his slow length curving round
And climb again the broken bank of my wall-face.

And as he put his head into that dreadful hole,
And as he slowly drew up, snake-easing his shoulders, and entered further,
A sort of horror, a sort of protest against his withdrawing into that horrid black hole,
Deliberately going into the blackness, and slowly drawing himself after,
Overcame me now his back was turned.

I looked round, I put down my pitcher,
I picked up a clumsy log
And threw it at the water-trough with a clatter.

I think it did not hit him;
But suddenly that part of him that was left behind convulsed in undignified haste,
Writhed like lightning, and was gone
Into the black hole, the earth-lipped fissure in the wall-front
At which, in the intense still noon, I stared with fascination.

And immediately I regretted it.
I thought how paltry, how vulgar, what a mean act!
I despised myself and the voices of my accursèd human education.

And I thought of the albatross,
And I wished he would come back, my snake.

For he seemed to me again like a king,
Like a king in exile, uncrowned in the underworld,
Now due to be crowned again.

And so, I missed my chance with one of the lords
Of life.
And I have something to expiate:
A pettiness.

D.H. Lawrence

I still hate snakes! D.H. Lawrence should have killed this thing from under dirt.

All too often I find myself repeating his confession for "I have something to expiate *(atone for)*, a pettiness."

How often one's peers, using "If you were a man" and "If you weren't afraid" as an argument, lead us into foolish acts.

D.H. Lawrence, employing his imagination, evokes an experience many share, that dangerous animals tend to be the most fascinating to watch—from a distance. If David Herbert Lawrence had been next to the venomous snake, self-defense would have kicked in and notions of poetry cast out!

***

Lord,

Our actions sometimes prove petty, especially when we tune in to hear our thoughts and realize what lurks behind our decisions. Your motive and action fuse as one: love for each individual. Please help me to employ love as even a small percent of my approach to others.

YESTERDAY, WHEN I WAS YOUNG

Yesterday when I was young,
The taste of life was sweet as rain upon my tongue,
I teased at life as if it were a foolish game,
The way the evening breeze may tease a candle flame;

The thousand dreams I dreamed, the splendid things I planned
I always built, alas, on weak and shifting sand;
I lived by night and shunned the naked light of day
And only now I see how the years ran away.

Yesterday when I was young,
So many drinking songs were waiting to be sung,
So many wayward pleasures lay in store for me
And so much pain my dazzled eyes refused to see,

I ran so fast that time and youth at last ran out,
I never stopped to think what life was all about
And ev'ry conversation I can now recall
Concerned itself with me, and nothing else at all.

Yesterday, the moon was blue,
And ev'ry crazy day brought something new to do,
I used my magic age as if it were a wand,
And never saw the waste and emptiness beyond;

The game of love I played with arrogance and pride
And ev'ry flame I lit too quickly, quickly died;
The friends I made all seemed somehow to drift away
And only I am left on stage to end the play.

There are so many songs in me that won't be sung,
I feel the bitter taste of tears upon my tongue,
The time has come for me to pay for Yesterday
When I was young.

Charles Aznavour

I enjoyed youth, only yesterday—invincible and proud. Am I wiser now, having made commitments, or simply aware we overlook the flaws of the young, but now no longer good looking and physically fit, I have only the grind of everyday existence to look forward to?

Let my children enjoy, but not waste, their youth. They do need to make commitments.

***

Lord,

Take away heavy burdens and let youths enjoy their days of less responsibility. Not to be frivolous, but spent in preparation for days ahead, at a slow pace!

You give us time to grow up and mature. To everything there comes a season. I pray I take advantage of opportunities I'm given every day and not find myself with few years left and tons of time wasted.

July 4

Independence Day

9:00

10:00

11:00

12:00

1:00

2:00

3:00

4:00   *Family picnic, fireworks at dusk*

5:00

Gregg Tomusko

AMERICA THE BEAUTIFUL

O beautiful for spacious skies,
  For amber waves of grain,
For purple mountain majesties
  Above the fruitful plain!
America! America!
  God shed his grace on thee,
And crown thy good with brotherhood
  From sea to shining sea!

O beautiful for pilgrim feet,
  Whose stern, impassioned stress
A thoroughfare for freedom beat
  Across the wilderness!
America! America!
  God mend thine every flaw,
Confirm thy soul in self-control,
  Thy liberty in law!

O beautiful for heroes proved
  In liberating strife,
Who more than self their country loved,
  And mercy more than life!
America! America!
  May God thy gold refine
Till all success be nobleness
  And every gain divine!

O beautiful for patriot dream
  That sees beyond the years
Thine alabaster cities gleam
  Undimmed by human tears!
America! America!
  God shed His grace on thee
And crown thy good with brotherhood
  From sea to shining sea!

Katharine Lee Bates

The best in America reflects the beauty of God, the majestic land, diversity of pristine national parks, unspoiled wilderness kept as the natives first gazed upon it, and worked soil.

The best in America practices God's truth, citing a history of stalwart souls who would not cave in to oppression, whose beliefs ran deeper than their comforts. Her crowning achievement comprises the development of law, of which good men willingly submit to allow all men freedom.

The best in America acts upon the goodness of God, keeping spiritual idealism alive, those who pray for brotherhood from sea to shining sea—all 360 degrees, spreading faith from the Pacific to the Atlantic and continuing from the Atlantic to the Pacific.

America compares to a well-nourished sapling growing tall beneath a golden sun.

***

Lord,

Bless this beautiful country with noble aspirations, desiring peace and good will to all men. We are great, because we've tried to do your will here on earth. Let us never lose your protection. We owe everything to you. Keep us one nation under God.

August   19

 9:00

10:00

11:00

12:00

 1:00   *Summer Picnic—Emerald Park*

 2:00

 3:00

 4:00

 5:00

CHILDREN

Come to me, O ye children!
   For I hear you at your play,
And the questions that perplexed me
   Have vanished quite away.

Ye open the eastern windows,
   That look towards the sun,
Where thoughts are singing swallows
   And the brooks of morning run.

In your hearts are the birds and the sunshine,
   In your thoughts the brooklet's flow,
But in mine is the wind of Autumn
   And the first fall of the snow.

Ah! what would the world be to us
   If the children were no more?
We should dread the desert behind us
   Worse than the dark before.

What the leaves are to the forest,
   With light and air for food,
Ere their sweet and tender juices
   Have been hardened into wood, –

That to the world are children;
   Through them it feels the glow
Of a brighter and sunnier climate
   Than reaches the trunks below.

Come to me, O ye children!
   And whisper in my ear
What the birds and the winds are singing
   In your sunny atmosphere.

For what are all our contrivings,
    And the wisdom of our books,
When compared with your caresses,
    And the gladness of your looks?

Ye are better than all the ballads
    That ever were sung or said;
For ye are living poems,
    And all the rest are dead.

Henry Wadsworth Longfellow

Henry Wadsworth Longfellow loves and appreciates children. Akin to dancing branches all around us and still connected to us older wood. Longfellow's comparisons flow as natural as water, simple yet profound. As the opposite of a parable offering a single meaning, these comparisons welcome further exploration, like the many paths that children create through the woods.

***

Jesus,

Bless the children. How they love you and want to hear your stories. You never send them away. You always take time for them, even when in the middle of a lesson.

Let us love and appreciate all children as you do.

ON HEARING A SYMPHONY OF BEETHOVEN

Sweet sounds, oh, beautiful music, do not cease!
Reject me not into the world again.
With you alone is excellence and peace,
Mankind made plausible, his purpose plain.
Enchanted in your air benign and shrewd,
With limbs a–sprawl and empty faces pale,
The spiteful and the stingy and the rude
Sleep like the scullions in the fairy-tale.

This moment is the best the world can give:
The tranquil blossom on the tortured stem.
Reject me not, sweet sounds; oh, let me live,
Till Doom espy my towers and scatter them,
A city spell-bound under the aging sun.
Music my rampart, and my only one.

Edna St. Vincent Millay

The sublimity of Beethoven's music expressed in words. Music and poetry excel as an expression of man's longing for something better—hopefully, our "next stop".

The opportunity today to bring a picnic basket full of delicious snacks and relax on a blanket in the grass beneath the stars and listen to a live performance of a world-class orchestra I consider something truly wonderful.

***

Lord,

Music provides a universal language. While we struggle to speak one language on our planet, through each other's compositions we experience unity. Help us to speak one language so we can begin to trust one another and have a chance at peace on earth.

End of Summer Discussion

The children will be back to school soon. Amazing, they can find almost every great song and poem on the internet, quickly, many displayed against a beautiful background, and some with accompanying information.

I know we missed a lot of favorites. Any you'd like to mention?

Good-Bye Now, Plato and Hegel from *"Autumn Journal"* by Louis MacNeice
_____

It ends up impractical to earn a liberal arts degree. It requires a lot of money and effort to secure a position in the unemployment line! And it remains one possession I value more each year as I grow older, because it contains lasting value.

It strikes me ironic that the education Louis MacNeice mocks serves as the very thing that enables his name to live on long after his death, for this poem we honor as a "keeper."

***

Father,

Thank you for the privilege of learning liberal arts; men and women who dedicated their lives to truth, beauty, and goodness. I was really learning about you.

The Unknown Citizen by W.H. Auden

Are we unknown citizens, doing what seems right, so engulfed in daily occupations and making decisions expected, so conditioned by society that we forget we are individuals?

***

Lord,

Like a patient kept alive by tubes, we merely exist. Where did the fire of the Holy Spirit go? Where the love that burns in our hearts? Help us to live a spiritual life, not merely do our duties. And keep our government lean, or the slob will crush us.

Soldier by George L. Skypeck

A man who served in Vietnam always kept this poem outside his office. He loves reading about the Civil War, an enthusiast and scholar who dons a Union uniform for battle reenactments. It occurs more often to hear him talk about the losses at Antietam than the communications cable he witnessed cut on Hamburger Hill.

I feel honored to be his friend.

***

Heavenly Father,

I should have gone. We all should have gone. Lord, when I'm provided an easy excuse to wash my hands of a bad situation, how quickly I become convinced. Give me the courage to do my duty, as a fool, as a follower of you.

A Carol for Children by Ogden Nash

The poisons we put in our lakes may ultimately leech down into the pure waters of our underground springs. When we've destroyed our children, when they become polluted, we have gone too far.

Christmas belongs to children of all ages. The world wishes to decrease the maximum allowable age of a child. Christ hopes to retain those qualities throughout our days.

We have gone too far. We have lost the infant Lord.

***

Heavenly Father,

Let us regain our faith. Trusting you makes our life worthwhile. Faith endures as the greatest gift we can give our children. Help us all to build a better world; for us and our children.

I Have Lighted the Candles, Mary by Kenneth Patchen

What a contrast between what we find in a good man's heart, and the world outside; a world gone mad with war, and the gentle breathing of a sleeping baby.

The child reminds us that the most malignant evil will be overcome by goodness.

***

Jesus,

You are our only hope. I pray all men feel the love you have for each of us. Give us spiritual strength and insight so we can transform our world, one individual at a time.

somewhere I have never travelled by E.E. Cummings

Knowing you encompasses an ineffable experience. Like traveling to a place I have never been, or a rose experiencing the wonder of spring, and sometimes a flower when unexpectedly the first snow begins to fall. Knowing you I appraise worth more than anything else I ever felt. Your breath descends gentle and absolute. You mean everything to me.

The inexpressible, expressed in a poem.

***

Lord,
There remained so much that you intended to teach us, but with our language limited and spiritual development retarded, you could not yet tell us.

Perhaps this poem touches upon things you wished to tell us but could not.

Dress Rehearsal Rag by Leonard Cohen

This seven-minute song revolves about a man contemplating suicide, again and again, like a dress rehearsal.

If images count as gold, this song could make us wealthy! The thoughts weave through dreams, then return to a life in ruins. All these snapshots of despair probably entered the mind in one flash-lit instant.

***

Heavenly Father,
Knowing what we could have been and where we are eats at our soul. Failure leaves a bitter taste. Life punches hard, and sometimes the world seems better off without us. Save us, Father. Help us to realize that no matter what, we look

precious in your eyes. We remain your sons and daughters.

What matters is that we love you.

Ballad of the Goodly Fere by Ezra Pound

Here we find a Jesus portrayed poles apart from our Hollywood movies and Sunday school teachings as a gentle, dreamy, sacrificial lamb. His apostle Simon, emboldened by the Spirit, remembers his master as a man who commanded each life situation. Strong, rugged laborers and the fiery nationalist Simon would not call a weakling "master." This man faced his enemies, and met death, even a cruel death, without fear. And he lives, as he said he would.

The language, words, and content make this an authentic-sounding speech that Simon Zelotes maybe delivered.

***

Jesus,

An eyewitness account from a close companion tells us, for the first time, what you were really like and how you braved the evil that men did to you. You were a hardworking layman who loved nature and harmed no man, but rather loved them, loved life from start to end, and continue to love us today.

As Ezra Pound suggests, books serve as no substitute to actually meeting someone and seeing what they're like. I hope to meet you, Jesus, one day face to face, and then get to know you even more personally.

When You Wish Upon A Star by Ned Washington and Leigh Harline

Walt Disney enhanced my childhood with wonder, excitement, and pure magic. He produced only the highest quality art, that which would please a perfectionist. Walt even risked bankruptcy for excellence. He sent artists to study deer in the forests, scrapping much of the original Bambi's footage, so the animation of the wildlife would look more natural.

A worry as a child came about when I and others wished for something, if it made a difference who we are. To angels, Walt Disney taught us, it doesn't matter who you are. Pinocchio *could* become a real boy.

Childhood provided a wonderful place to be when Jiminy Cricket sang with an angelic voice to a heavenly melody these words that we all hope are true.

***

Heavenly Father,

I used to lie on our clubhouse roof and look up at the night sky. What a vast universe filled with wonder. How small we really must be.

We would wish upon the "first star we see tonight", and be thrilled to see a falling star. Maybe all of my wishes came true, as I can no longer remember what I wished for.

We can go on all night. Let the fire burn while we get some rest.

EPILOGUE

I keep finding more great lyrics and poems!

I watched the Al Jolson Story and for the first time heard the lyrics to "The Anniversary Waltz," one of my favorite tunes I played on the piano. The lyrics matched the beauty of the melody.

I heard a song, "Walk With Me" (if that's the title) once at the Neumann Club at Cleveland State University many years ago. It has always stayed with me. I never heard it again. I cannot find anyone who's ever heard it.

I did not want this song to be lost forever. If it had been in a book, it would be whole. I guess that's what books are for. A remnant from my memory goes:

WALK WITH ME

Walk with me, talk with me,
Tell me of the good things you've done.
Stay with me, pray with me,
Leave your blues in your shoes at my door.

I was a young man once, I know it
My mother has pictures to show it
She always knew I'd outgrow it
I guess that's what pictures are for.

And it's
Walk with me, talk with me,
Tell me of the good things you've done.
Stay with me, pray with me,
Leave your blues in your shoes at my door.

I went to school for a long time
Expecting to stay in a straight line
Then I found that the great minds
Don't stay in a straight line at all

And it's
Walk with me, talk with me,
Tell me of the good things you've done.
Stay with me, pray with me,
Leave your blues in your shoes at my door.

(lost stanza)
I live in a house, …
Four walls and a ceiling….

(Do not know author)

After years of searching, a friend found the song for me. Three cheers for the Internet. Four cheers for a friend, especially one who can successfully search the Internet!

STAY WITH ME

I am a man without envy
No roof and no walls to defend me
In hope that someday you'll defend me
And take all my troubles away

Refrain:
Walk with me, talk with me
Tell me about all the good things you've done
Stay with me, pray with me
Leave all your blues in your shoes at the door

I went to school for a long time
Expecting to stay in a straight line
Until I discovered that great minds
Don't stay in a straight line at all

Refrain

Gregg Tomusko

I was a child once, I know it
My mother has pictures to show it
But she always knew I'd outgrow it
I guess that's what pictures are for

Erich Sylvester

THE END

In the end, we find Christ or perish. Poetry does not suffice. But revealing Christ through a poem or song sure looks good on our soul's "resume"!

On the invitation we get from God, we must R.S.V.P. by prayer.

I hope these poems, songs, and prayers continue to bring us all closer to God. "May the good Lord bless and keep you."

Sincerely,
A fellow traveler

Index by Title

Index by Author

Bibliography

(The) Book of Hymns, edited by Ian Bradley. Woodstock, New York: The Overlook Press, 1989.

Newton, John and John P. Rees (last verse). *Amazing Grace.*

(The) Cambridge Edition of the Letters and Works of D.H. Lawrence, THE POEMS VOLUME I, edited by Christopher Pollnitz. Cambridge CB2 8BS, United Kingdom: Cambridge University Press, University Printing House, 2013. © copyright 2013 Cambridge University.

Cohen, Leonard

Cohen, Leonard. *Selected Poems 1956-1968*, from *The Spice-Box of Earth*. New York, New York: Penquin Books, 625 Madison Avenue, 1978.

Song

Leonard Cohen songs and Quotes from Leonard Cohen songs

Cohen, Leonard. *Leonard Cohen – Stranger Music – Selected Poems and Songs*. New York, New York: Vintage Books, A Division of Random House, Inc., 1994.

Cohen, Leonard. *Anthem.*

   Copyright 1992 by Stranger Music, Inc. (BMI), New York.

Cohen, Leonard. *Bird on the Wire.*

   Copyright 1968, 1969 by Stranger Music, Inc. (BMI), New York.

Cohen, Leonard. *Suzanne.*

   Copyright 1966 by Project Seven Music, New York.

Cohen, Leonard. *Take This Waltz.*

   Copyright 1988 by CBS Records, Inc.

Cohen, Leonard. *The Future.*

   Copyright 1992 by Leonard Cohen Stranger Music, Inc. (BMI), New York.

Dinner Reservation: Leonard Cohen

Quotes of Leonard Cohen

Cohen, Leonard. *The Spice-Box of Earth*. New York, New York: The Viking Press, Inc., 625 Madison Avenue, 10022, 1965.

Cohen, Leonard. *Book of Mercy*. New York: Villard Books, a division of Random House, Inc., 1984.

Recommended Resources

Cohen, Leonard. *Leonard Cohen, I'm Your Man*, a film by Lian Lunson, @ 2006 Lions Gate Films, Inc., Lionsgate, 2700 Colorado Avenue, Santa Monica, California 90404.

Tribute concert January, 2005.

Cohen, Leonard. Austin City Limits, *Leonard Cohen in Concert* (with Christie Albert and Paul Glasse).

Corbett, Brother Thomas, S.M. and Reverend William J. Boldt. *Modern American Poetry*. New York: The Macmillan Company, 1965.

Masters, Edgar Lee. *Lucinda Matlock* from *Spoon River Anthology*.

Cummings, E.E.

COMPLETE POEMS: 1904-1962 by E E. Cummings, edited by George J. Firmage. Liveright Publishing Corporation, 500 Fifth Avenue, New York, N.Y. 10110. W,W, Norton & Company Ltd., 10 Coptic Street, London WE1A 1PU.

Dickinson, Emily

Dinner Reservation: Emily Dickinson

Letters of Emily Dickinson

Dickinson, Emily. *Open Me Carefully, Emily Dickinson's Intimate Letters to Susan Huntington Dickinson*, Edited by Ellen Louise Hart and Martha Neil Smith. Copyright @ 1998, Paris Press, P.O. Box 487, Ashfield, MA, 01330.

Emily Dickinson poems and Quotes from Emily Dickinson poems

www.online-literature.com/dickinson

/poems-series-1/, /poems-series-2/, and /poems-series-3/

or: Dickinson, Emily, *Emily Dickinson Poems*, Lowe & B. Hould Publishers, an imprint of Borders, Inc., 311 Maynard, Ann Arbor, MI 48104, first published in 1890, Edited by two of her friends Mabel Loomis Todd and T.W. Higginson

Note: Original dashes and capitalizations removed for a more standard look of a poem.

I Died for Beauty	Series 1, IV. Time and Eternity, X
I Never Saw a Moor	Series 1, I. Life, XVII
I'm Nobody	Series 2, I. Life, I
Success Is Counted Sweetest	Series 1, I. Life, I

| The Chariot | Series 1, IV. Time and Eternity, XXVII |
| The Snake | Series 2, III. Nature, XXIV |

//en.wikisource.org/wiki/ for

"Morning" — means "Milking" — to the Farmer — and

"Nature" is what we see

Dylan, Bob

Dylan, Bob. *Lyrics, 1962-1985.* New York: Alfred A. Knopf, 1990.

Dylan, Bob. *Forever Young.*

   Copyright 1973, 1974 by Ram's Horn Music.

Dylan, Bob. *I Dreamed I Saw St. Augustine.*

   Copyright 1968 by Dwarf Music.

Dylan, Bob. *My Back Pages.*

   Copyright 1964 by Warner Bros. Inc.

Dylan, Bob. *To Ramona.*

   Copyright 1964 by Warner Bros. Inc.

Dylan, Bob. *When the Ship Comes In.*

   Copyright 1963, 1964 by Warner Bros. Inc.

Eliot, T. S.

Dinner Reservation: T. S. Eliot

Quotes from T. S. Eliot *Selected Essays*

Eliot, T.S. *Selected Essays.* Orlando, Florida: Harcourt Brace Jovanovich, Inc., Copyright 1950, 1936, 1932, Publishers, 32887.

Quotes from T. S. Eliot *On Poetry and Poets*

Eliot, T.S. *On Poetry and Poets.* New York: Farrar, Straus and Cudahy, 1957.

Quotes from T. S. Eliot *Notes towards the Definition of Culture*

Eliot, T.S. *Notes towards the Definition of Culture.* New York: Harcourt, Brace and Company, Copyright, 1949, by T.S. Eliot.

Quotes from T. S. Eliot *The Idea of a Christian Society*

Eliot, T.S. *The Idea of a Christian Society.* New York: Harcourt, Brace and Company. Copyright, 1940, by T. S .Eliot.

Quotes from T. S. Eliot *After Strange Gods, A Primer of Modern Heresy*

Eliot, T. S. *After Strange Gods, A Primer of Modern Heresy*, The Page-Barbour Lectures at The University of Virginia 1933, New York: Harcourt, Brace and Company.

T. S. Eliot poems and

(Select) Quotes from T. S. Eliot plays and Quotes from T. S. Eliot poems

Eliot, T.S. *The Complete Poems and Plays, 1909-1950.* Orlando, Florida: Harcourt Brace & Company, 6277 Sea Harbor Drive, 32887-6777.

Gabriel, Brigitte. *They Must Be Stopped. Why We Must Defeat Radical Islam. How We Can Do It.*

New York, New York: St. Martin's Press, 175 Fifth Avenue, 10010.

Hopkins, Gerard Manley

Dinner Reservation: Gerard Manley Hopkins

Quotes of Gerard Manly Hopkins

Hopkins, Gerard Manley. *Mortal Beauty, God's Grace, Major Poems and Spiritual Writings of Gerard Manley Hopkins,* edited by John F. Thornton and Susan B. Varenne. Vintage Spiritual Classics. Copyright @ 2003 by Random House, Inc., New York.

Pick, John. *Gerard Manley Hopkins Priest and Poet.* A Galaxy Book, Oxford University Press, 1966.

Quotes from Gerard Manly Hopkins poems

Hopkins, Gerard Manley. *Mortal Beauty, God's Grace, Major Poems and Spiritual Writings of Gerard Manley Hopkins,* edited by John F. Thornton and Susan B. Varenne. Vintage Spiritual Classics. Copyright @ 2003 by Random House, Inc., New York.

Ideals, Easter Issue, Vol 27, No. 2 - March 1970. Milwaukee, Wisconsin: Published Bimonthly by Ideals Publishing Co., 11315 Watertown Plank Road, 53226.

Nedrow, Ella Castle. *Easter Symbol.*

Kristofferson, Kris

The Songs of Kris Kristofferson, Chappell Music Company, Harper & Row, Publishers, Inc.

Kristofferson, Kris. *Jody and the Kid.*

Copyright 1968 by Buckhorn Music Publishers, Inc., (BMI).

Kristofferson, Kris. *Loving Her Was Easier.*

Copyright 1970 by Combine Music Corp.

Kristofferson, Kris. *Silver (The Hunger)*.

　　Copyright 1975 by Resaca Music Publishing Co. (BMI).

Kristofferson, Kris. *Sunday Mornin' Comin' Down*.

　　Copyright by Monument Record Corporation.

Kristofferson, Kris. *The Pilgrim: Chapter 33*.

　　Copyright 1970 by Combine Music Corp. Used by permission.

Kristofferson, Kris. *Vietnam Blues*.

　　Copyright 1965 by Buckhorn Music Publishers, Inc.

Dinner Reservation: Kris Kristofferson

Recommended Resources

Kristofferson Special, Disney Channel 8/1995.

Willie Nelson Presents the Veteran of the Year Award to Kris Kristofferson
http://www.liveleak.com/view?i=1b8_1331866375

(A) Little Treasury of Modern Poetry, edited by Oscar Williams. New York: Charles Scribner's Sons, Inc., 1952.

Millay, Edna St. Vincent. *On Hearing a Symphony of Beethoven*.

Yeats, W.B. *An Irish Airman Foresees His Death*.

Longfellow, Henry Wadsworth

Longfellow, Henry Wadsworth. *The Poetical Works of Longfellow*. Massachusetts: Cambridge Edition, Houghton Mifflin Company Boston. Copyright @ 1975, 2 Park Street, Boston, Massachusetts 02108.

Dinner Reservation: Henry Wadsworth Longfellow

Quotes of Henry Wadsworth Longfellow

Longfellow, Henry Wadsworth. *Poems and other Writings*. J. D. McClatchy, copyright @ 2000 by Literary Classics for the United States, Inc., New York, N.Y. Distributed by Penguin Putnam, Inc.

Quotes of Henry Wadsworth Longfellow (*about poems*)

Longfellow, Henry Wadsworth. *The Poetical Works of Longfellow*. Massachusetts: Cambridge Edition, Houghton Mifflin Company Boston. Copyright @ 1975, 2 Park Street, Boston, Massachusetts 02108.

Quotes from Henry Wadsworth Longfellow poems

Longfellow, Henry Wadsworth. *The Poetical Works of Longfellow.* Massachusetts: Cambridge Edition, Houghton Mifflin Company Boston. Copyright @ 1975, 2 Park Street, Boston, Massachusetts 02108.

(The) New Ultimate Country Fake-Book, Winona, Minnesota: Hal Leonard Publishing Corporation, 960 East Mark Street, 1986.

Aznavour , Charles. *Yesterday, When I Was Young.*

   Copyright 1965 and 1966 by Editiones Musicales Charles Aznavour, Paris, France.

      TRO - Hampshire House Publishing Corp., New York, controls all publication rights for the USA. and Canada.

Clark, Guy. *Desperados Waiting for the Train.*

   Copyright 1973 by Sunberry Music, Inc.

   All rights assigned to Chappell & Co., Inc.

Hall, Tom T. *Old Dogs, Children and Watermelon Wine.*

   Copyright 1972 by Hallnote Music, Nashville, TN.

(The) Norton Anthology of English Literature, Volume 1. New York: W.W.Norton & Company, Inc., 1962.

Shakespeare, William. *Sonnet 29* (When, in disgrace with fortune).

Shakespeare, William. *Sonnet 73* (That time of year thou mayst in me behold).

(The) Norton Anthology of English Literature, Volume 2. New York, New York: W.W.Norton & Company, Inc., 1968.

Arnold, Matthew. *Dover Beach.*

Hopkins, Gerard Manley. *Binsey Poplars.*

Hopkins, Gerard Manley. *God's Grandeur.*

Hopkins, Gerard Manley. *Spring.*

Hopkins, Gerard Manley. *The Windhover.*

Hopkins, Gerard Manley. *Thou Art Indeed Just, Lord.*

Keats, John. *On First Looking into Chapman's Homer.*

Landor, Walter Savage. *On His Seventy-fifth Birthday.*

Wordsworth, William. *She Dwelt Among the Untrodden Ways.*

Wordsworth, William. *The World Is Too Much With Us.*

Yeats, W.B. *The Lake Isle of Innisfree*.

Yeats, W.B. *The Old Men Admiring Themselves in the Water*.

Yeats, W.B. *The Second Coming*.

Yeats, W.B. *The Wild Swans at Coole*.

Yeats, W.B. *When You Are Old*.

100 Poems by 100 Poets, selected by Harold Pinter. New York, New York: Geoffrey Godbert and Anthony Astbury, Grove Press, Inc., 1987.

Rossetti, Christina. *What Would I Give?*.

(The) Oxford Book of Christmas Poems, edited by Michael Harrison and Christopher Stuart-Clark. Oxford: Oxford University Press, Walton Street, 1983.

Moore, Clement Clark. *A Visit from St Nicholas*.

(The) Pocket Book of Verse, Great English and American Poems, by M.Edmund Speare. New York, New York: Pocket Books, Inc., 1230 Sixth Avenue.

Field, Eugene. *Little Boy Blue*.

Hood, Thomas. *I Remember, I Remember*.

Robinson, Edward Arlington. *Miniver Cheevy*.

Robinson, Edward Arlington. *Richard Cory*.

Whitman, Walt. *When I Heard the Learn'd Astronomer*.

Poems of Christmas, Edited by Myra Cohn Livingston. "A Margaret K. McElderry Book," Atheneum, 1980.

Behn, Harry. *A Christmas Carol*.

Poems of Praise, selected and illustrated by Pelagie Doane. Philadelphia and New York: J.B. Lippincott Company, 1955.

Untermeyer, Louis. *Spanish Lullaby*.

Poetry Festival, edited by John Bettenbender. New York, New York: Dell Publishing Co., Inc., 1966.

Hunt, James Henry Leigh. *Abou Ben Adhem*.

Seasonal Missalette, Vol. 11, No. 6: March 31, 1996, World Library Publications, a division of J.S.Paluch Company, Inc., P.O.Box 2703, Schiller Park, IL 60176.

Deiss, Lucien, CSSp. (1921-2007)   *Keep in Mind.* @1965, 1966, World Library Publications, Inc.

Gabarain, Cesareo. *Lord, When You Came.* @1979, 1987, Cesareo Gabarain, Published by OCP.

Were You There. Negro Spiritual.

(The) Treasury of Christian Poetry, Compiled by Lorraine Eitel. Old Tappan, New Jersey: Fleming H. Revell Company, 1982.

The Guest. Anonymous.

Wilkin, Marijohn

Wilkin, Marijohn & Kris Kristofferson. *One Day at a Time.*

   Copyright 1973 by Buckhorn Music Publishers, Inc.

Wise, Joe

Wise, Joe. *Lord, Teach Us to Pray.*

   Copyright 1994 GIA Publications, Inc. 7404 S. Mason Ave., Chicago, IL 60638.

Woods, Ralph L. *Famous Poems and the Little-Known Stories Behind Them.* New York: Hawthorn Books, Inc., 1961.

Bates, Katharine Lee. *America the Beautiful.*

Howe, Julia Ward. *The Battle Hymn of the Republic.*

Mohr, Joseph. *Silent Night.*

Yeats, W.B.

Dinner Reservation: William Butler Yeats

Quotes from W.B. Yeats

Yeats, W.B. *The Yeats Reader, A Portable Compendium of Poetry, Drama, and Prose*, Edited by Richard J. Finneran. New York, New York: Scribner Poetry, Scribner, 1230 Avenue of the Americas, 10020.

Quotes from W.B. Yeats letters

Yeats, W.B. *The Collected Letters of W.B. Yeats, Volume I, 1865-1895*, edited by John Kelly. Oxford: Clarendon Press, 1986 and Oxford University Press, Walton Street, OX2 6DP.

Yeats, W.B. *The Collected Letters of W.B. Yeats, Volume II, 1896-1900*, edited by Warwick Gould, John Kelly, Deirdre Toomey. Oxford: Clarendon Press and Oxford University Press, Great Clarendon Street, OX2 6DP.

Yeats, W.B. *The Collected Letters of W.B. Yeats, Volume III, 1901-1904*, edited by John Kelly and Ronald Schuchard. Oxford: Clarendon Press, 1994, Oxford University Press, Walton Street, OX2 6DP

Yeats, W.B. *The Collected Letters of W.B. Yeats, Volume IV, 1905-1907*, edited by John Kelly and Ronald Schuchard. Oxford: Oxford University Press, Great Clarendon Street, OX2 6DP.

Quotes from W. B. Yeats poems

Yeats, W.B. *The Collected Poems of W.B. Yeats*, Edited by Richard J. Finneran. New York, New York: Scribner Paperback Poetry, Simon & Schuster Inc., Rockefeller Center, 1230 Avenue of the Americas, 10020.

(Do not know the Source)

Robbins, Mary Loveridge. *Parent's Prayer.*

Copyright Permissions

Selected lines from various T.S. Eliot Poems, including lines from On Poetry and Poets

Selected lines from various T.S. Eliot Works,

Masters, Edgar Lee *Lucinda Matlock*
"Lucinda Matlock" from *Spoon River Anthology* by Edgar Lee Masters. Reprinted by permission of the estate of Hilary Masters.

Millay, Edna St. Vincent *On Hearing a Symphony of Beethoven*
Edna St. Vincent Millay, Millay "On Hearing a Symphony of Beethoven" from *Collected Poems*. Copyright 1928, © 1955 by Edna St. Vincent Millay and Norma Millay Ellis. Reprinted with the permission of The Permissions Company, Inc., on behalf of Holly Peppe, Literary Executor, The Millay Society.www.millay.org.

Wilkin, Marijohn & Kris Kristofferson   *One Day at a Time*
One Day at a Time written by Marijohn Wilkin and Kris Kristofferson. Copyright 1973 by Buckhorn Music Publishers, Inc. Reprinted with the permission of John Wilkin on behalf of Buckhorn Music Publishers. All Rights Reserved.

Wise, Joe *Lord, Teach Us to Pray*
"Lord, Teach Us to Pray" by Joe Wise
Copyright © 1971, 1972 by GIA Publications, Inc.,www.giamusic.com
All rights reserved. Used by permission.

Yeats, W.B.   Quotes from W.B. Yeats letters
Quotations totaling 360 words (pp. 33,164,202-203,234,255,338,404,437-438) from *The Collected Letters of W.B. Yeats, Volume I, 1865-1895* edited by John Kelly (1986). By permission of Oxford University Press. (URL www.oup.com)

Made in the USA
Columbia, SC
02 February 2020